UNITED NATIONS AT A GLANCE

United Nations at a Glance

Published by the United Nations

New York, New York 10017, United States of America

ISBN: 978-92-1-101252-1

eISBN: 978-92-1-055135-9

United Nations Publication

Sales No. E.11.I.16

Design and layout

Outreach Division, Department of Public Information,

United Nations, New York

CONTENTS

CHAPTER 1

AN INTRODUCTION
TO THE UNITED NATIONS

QUICK FACTS
ABOUT THE UNITED NATIONS

The United Nations was initially conceived as a wartime alliance on 1 January 1942 and established as an international organization on 24 October 1945. To commemorate the creation of the United Nations, the world celebrates **United Nations Day** each year on 24 October.

———————————

The United Nations has **four purposes**: (1) to maintain international peace and security; (2) to develop friendly relations among nations; (3) to cooperate in solving international problems and promoting respect for human rights; and (4) to be a centre for harmonizing the actions of nations. More than 30 affiliated organizations cooperate in this effort. They are known together as the **United Nations System**, and all have their own specific areas of work.

———————————

The United Nations is **not a world government**. However, it does provide the means to help resolve international conflicts and formulate policies on matters affecting all of us. The United Nations is a forum where all countries meet to discuss, elaborate and extend international law in areas such as human rights, international trade, the sea, and the fight against terrorism.

———————————

At the United Nations, all the Member States—large and small, rich and poor, with differing political views and social systems—have a voice and a vote in making decisions in the **General Assembly**.

———————————

The United Nations System works to promote respect for human rights, reduce poverty, fight disease and protect the environment. The United Nations leads **international campaigns** against drug trafficking and terrorism, as well as to eliminate violence against women and to protect natural ecosystems.

———————————

The United Nations and its agencies undertake a myriad of **projects throughout the world**, including assisting refugees; fighting AIDS; expanding food production; and providing help after natural disasters.

———————————

CHAPTER 1
AN INTRODUCTION TO THE UNITED NATIONS

HISTORY

THE IDEA OF A PEACEFUL WORLD COMMUNITY

Although the United Nations came into being during the Second World War (1939-1945), the ideal of a community of nations living in peace was conceived much earlier. Back in 1795, the German philosopher Immanuel Kant developed the idea of perpetual peace, a doctrine based on what we now call the rule of law. He advocated that nations establish a peaceful world community, not through a global government, but with each country becoming a free State respectful of its citizens and foreign visitors, thus promoting a peaceful society worldwide.

With this idea, Kant not only influenced philosophical and political thinking, he also sparked the development of international law and the creation of institutions such as the Inter-Parliamentary Union (established in 1889, a forerunner to the League of Nations and, today, a Permanent Observer at the United Nations). His influence is likewise clearly visible in the "Fourteen Points" speech given by American President Woodrow Wilson to the United States Congress on 8 January 1918, which included the first mention of the League of Nations.

THE LEAGUE OF NATIONS

The League of Nations was set up in 1919, following the First World War. It was officially established when 44 countries signed the Covenant of the League of Nations, part I of the Treaty of Versailles.

The main objective of the League of Nations was to keep world peace by promoting disarmament, preventing war through collective security, settling disputes between countries through negotiation and diplomacy and improving global welfare.

However, the League had certain fundamental weaknesses. If States involved in a dispute chose to ignore the League's decisions, the League could introduce economic sanctions; since it did not have a military force, it had no way of enforcing those decisions.

In addition, not all countries were members of the League of Nations. The United States, for example, was never a member, despite President Wilson's efforts and involvement in the League's creation. Other States that had joined later quit, and the League often failed to take action when necessary.

Despite these weaknesses, the League of Nations was able to resolve some disputes and stop some small wars. It successfully intervened in the dispute between Sweden and Finland over the Aaland Islands (1921) and stopped Greece's invasion of Bulgaria (1925). However, it was ineffective in preventing or stopping powerful nations from fighting. When Italy invaded Abyssinia (Ethiopia) in 1935, the League condemned the act of aggression and imposed sanctions, but the sanctions had no impact. Moreover, the League was powerless in the face of events leading up to the Second World War.

The League of Nations at its opening session in Geneva.

Though it did not succeed, the League of Nations initiated the dream of a universal organization. Its successor was the United Nations, which inherited the assets and property of the dissolved League, worth approximately US$22 million in 1946, including the Palais des Nations in Geneva (Switzerland) and the League's archives.

CREATION OF THE UNITED NATIONS

The idea of the United Nations was born during the Second World War. Allied world leaders who had collaborated to end the war felt a strong need for a mechanism that would help bring peace and stop future wars. They realized that this was possible only if all nations worked together through a global organization. The United Nations was to be that organization.

Declaration of St. James's Palace

In June 1941, London was the home of nine exiled governments. The resilient British capital had already been through months of war, and in the bomb-marked city, air-raid sirens wailed all too frequently. Practically all of Europe had fallen to the Axis Powers and ships on the Atlantic carrying vital supplies sank with grim regularity. But in London itself and among the Allied governments and peoples faith in the ultimate victory remained unshaken.

On 12 June 1941, representatives of Great Britain, Canada, Australia, New Zealand and the Union of South Africa; the exiled governments of Belgium, Czechoslovakia, Greece, Luxembourg, the Netherlands, Norway, Poland and Yugoslavia; and General de Gaulle, leader of the Free French, met at the ancient St. James's Palace and signed a declaration, which states:

> "The only true basis of enduring peace is the willing cooperation of free peoples in a world in which, relieved of the menace of aggression, all may enjoy economic and social security; It is our intention to work together, and with other free peoples, both in war and peace, to this end."
>
> *—Declaration of St. James's Palace*

The Atlantic Charter

Two months later, United States President Franklin D. Roosevelt and British Prime Minister Winston Churchill met somewhere at sea—the same sea on which the desperate Battle of the Atlantic was being fought—and on 14 August 1941, issued a joint declaration known in history as the Atlantic Charter.

NOBODY EVER SIGNED THE ATLANTIC CHARTER

No signed version of the Atlantic Charter ever existed. It took several drafts before the British War Cabinet and Washington telegraphed each other the final agreed-upon text.

At a press conference in December 1944, United States President Roosevelt admitted that "nobody signed the Atlantic Charter." In British Prime Minister Churchill's account of the Yalta Conference, he quotes Roosevelt as saying, of the unwritten British constitution, "it was like the Atlantic Charter—the document did not exist, yet all the world knew about it."

In eight main points, the Atlantic Charter outlined a vision for a post-war settlement:

1. No territorial gains were to be sought by the United States or the United Kingdom.

2. Territorial adjustments must be in accord with the wishes of the peoples concerned.

3. All peoples had a right to self-determination.

4. Trade barriers were to be lowered.

5. There was to be global economic cooperation and advancement of social welfare.

6. Participants would work for a world free of want and fear.

7. Participants would work for freedom of the seas.

8. There was to be disarmament of aggressor nations and a post-war common disarmament.

It should be noted that the document emphasized that both "victor [and] vanquished" would be given market access "on equal terms". This was a direct refusal to weaken the defeated nations' economies with punitive sanctions, like those that had been imposed on Germany after the First World War and that are believed to have been partially responsible for igniting the Second World War.

At the subsequent meeting of the Inter-Allied Council in St. James' Palace in London on 24 September 1941, the governments of Belgium, Czechoslovakia, Greece, Luxembourg, the Netherlands, Norway, Poland, the Soviet Union, Yugoslavia and representatives of General de Gaulle unanimously adopted adherence to the common principles of policy set forth in the Atlantic Charter.

Declaration by United Nations

On New Year's Day 1942, representatives of the United States, the United Kingdom, the Soviet Union and China signed a short document known as the Declaration by United Nations. The next day, representatives of 22 other nations added their signatures. This important document pledged the signatory governments to the maximum war effort and bound them against making a separate peace.

Three years later, when preparations were being made for the San Francisco Conference, only those States that had declared war on the Axis powers and subscribed to the Declaration by United Nations by March 1945 were invited to take part.

Signing of the Declaration by United Nations (1 January 1942).

WE CAN BUILD A BETTER WORLD

"The Charter of the United Nations which you have just signed is a solid structure upon which we can build a better world. History will honour you for it. Between the victory in Europe and the final victory, in this most destructive of all wars, you have won a victory against war itself. [...] With this Charter the world can begin to look forward to the time when all worthy human beings may be permitted to live decently as free people.

"If we fail to use it, we shall betray all those who have died so that we might meet here in freedom and safety to create it. If we seek to use it selfishly—for the advantage of any one nation or any small group of nations—we shall be equally guilty of that betrayal."

> — *Harry S. Truman, President of the United States of America, at the San Francisco Conference*

Moscow and Tehran Conferences

By 1943, the Allies were committed to creating a world in which people "in all lands may live out their lives in freedom from fear and want." But the basis for a world organization had yet to be defined. On 30 October 1943, Vyaches Molotov, Anthony Eden and Cordell Hull—foreign ministers of, respectively, the Soviet Union, Great Britain and the United States—together with Foo Ping Shen, the Chinese Ambassador to the Soviet Union, signed the Moscow Declaration, which "recognizes the necessity of establishing at the earliest practicable date a general international organization, based on the principle of the sovereign equality of all peace-loving States, and open to membership by all such States, large and small, for the maintenance of international peace and security."

In December 1943, the American, British and Soviet leaders, Roosevelt, Churchill and Stalin, met in Tehran, the capital of Iran, and declared that they had worked out concerted plans for final victory.

Dumbarton Oaks and Yalta

The principles of the world organization-to-be were thus laid down. The structure was discussed at a business-like conference at Dumbarton Oaks (Washington, D.C.) in the autumn of 1944 by representatives of China, Great Britain, the Soviet Union and the United States. On 7 October 1944, the four powers submitted a proposal for the framework of the world organization to all the United Nations governments and to the peoples of all countries for their study and discussion.

According to the Dumbarton Oaks proposals, four main bodies were to constitute the organization to be known as the United Nations:

>> a General Assembly composed of all the members, with an Economic and Social Council working under its authority

>> a Security Council of 11 members, five permanent and six chosen from the remaining members by the General Assembly to hold office for two years

>> an International Court of Justice

>> a Secretariat

The essence of the plan was that the Security Council will be responsible for preventing future wars. The General Assembly will study, discuss and make recommendations in order to promote international cooperation and adjust situations likely to impair welfare. It will consider problems of cooperation in maintaining peace and security, and disarmament, in their general principles. However, it will not make recommendations on any matter being considered by the Security Council, and all questions on which action would become necessary must be referred to the Security Council.

Another important feature of the Dumbarton Oaks plan was that Member States were to place armed forces at the disposal of the Security Council in its task of preventing war and suppressing acts of aggression. The absence of such force, the organizers generally agreed, had been a fatal weakness in the League of Nations machinery for preserving peace.

The actual method of voting in the Security Council—an all-important question—was left open at Dumbarton Oaks for future discussion. It was taken up at Yalta (Crimea), where Churchill, Roosevelt and Stalin, together with their foreign ministers and chiefs of staff, again met in conference. On 11 February 1945, they announced that this question had been resolved and summoned the San Francisco Conference.

The San Francisco Conference: towards world peace

In the spring of 1945, delegates from 50 nations gathered in San Francisco. They represented over 80 per cent of the world's population and were determined to set up an organization that would preserve peace and help build a better world.

The main objective of the San Francisco Conference was to produce a document acceptable to all countries that would guide the work of the new organization.

?   DID YOU KNOW?

THE TERM "UNITED NATIONS" WAS FIRST USED BY AN AMERICAN PRESIDENT

The name "United Nations" was suggested by United States President Franklin D. Roosevelt. It was first officially used in 1942, when representatives of 26 countries signed the Declaration by United Nations. As a tribute to President Roosevelt, who died a few weeks before the signing of the Charter, all those present at the San Francisco Conference agreed to adopt the name "United Nations."

The Charter, the guiding principles of the United Nations, was signed on 26 June 1945, by the representatives of these 50 countries.

Poland was not represented at the Conference because at that time the country did not yet have a new government in place. However, Poland signed the Charter by 15 October 1945 and is therefore considered one of the original Members of the United Nations.

The 51 original Members States were (in alphabetical order, using the names of the countries as they were known in October 1945):

1. Argentina
2. Australia
3. Belgium
4. Bolivia
5. Brazil
6. Byelorussian Soviet Socialist Republic
7. Canada
8. Chile
9. China
10. Colombia
11. Costa Rica
12. Cuba
13. Czechoslovakia
14. Denmark
15. Dominican Republic
16. Ecuador
17. Egypt
18. El Salvador
19. Ethiopia
20. France
21. Greece
22. Guatemala
23. Haiti
24. Honduras
25. India
26. Iran
27. Iraq
28. Lebanon
29. Liberia
30. Luxembourg
31. Mexico
32. Netherlands
33. New Zealand
34. Nicaragua
35. Norway
36. Panama
37. Paraguay
38. Peru
39. Philippine Republic
40. Poland
41. Saudi Arabia
42. Syria
43. Turkey
44. Ukrainian Soviet Socialist Republic
45. Union of South Africa
46. Union of Soviet Socialist Republics (USSR)
47. United Kingdom (UK)
48. United States of America (USA)
49. Uruguay
50. Venezuela
51. Yugoslavia

After the represented countries, including the five permanent members of the Security Council (China, France, USA, UK and USSR), signed the Charter of the United Nations and officially recognized it, the United Nations came into being on 24 October 1945.

WHAT IS THE UNITED NATIONS?

The United Nations is a unique organization composed of independent countries that have come together to work for world peace and social progress. The Organization formally came into existence with just 51 countries. By 2012, the membership of the United Nations had grown to 193 countries.

FOCUS ON

THE ROAD TO THE UNITED NATIONS

28 June 1919	Creation of the League of Nations
3 September 1939	Poland invaded: Britain and France declare war on German Reich
7 December 1941	Attack on Pearl Harbour: the United States of America joins the Allies
12 June 1941	Declaration of St. James's Palace
14 August 1941	Adoption of the Atlantic Charter
1–2 January 1942	Declaration by United Nations
October-December 1943	Moscow and Tehran Conferences
Summer/autumn 1944	Dumbarton Oaks proposals
11 February 1945	Yalta Conference
8 May 1945	Allied victory in Europe proclaimed
26 June 1945	Adoption of the Charter of the United Nations at San Francisco Conference
24 October 1945	Creation of the United Nations
10 January 1946	First session of the United Nations General Assembly in London with representatives of 51 nations
12 April 1946	Final meeting and dissolution of the League of Nations

Since its inception, no country has ever been expelled from the United Nations. Indonesia temporarily quit the Organization in 1965 over a dispute with neighbouring Malaysia but returned the following year.

A FORUM FOR ALL COUNTRIES, NOT A WORLD GOVERNMENT

Governments represent countries and peoples. The United Nations represents neither a particular government nor any one nation. It represents all its Members and does only what the Member States decide that it should do.

GUIDING PRINCIPLES OF THE UNITED NATIONS

The Charter of the United Nations is the founding document guiding all of its under-takings. It is a set of guidelines that explains the rights and duties of each Member country and what needs to be done to achieve the goals they have set for themselves. When a nation becomes a Member of the United Nations, it accepts the aims and rules of the Charter.

EMBLEM

The original emblem was designed for the San Francisco Conference. After slight modifications, it was approved on 7 December 1946 as the emblem of the United Nations.

 **DID YOU KNOW?**

THE UNITED NATIONS HAS FOUR MAIN PURPOSES:

» to keep peace throughout the world

» to develop friendly relations among nations

» to work together to improve the lives of poor people, to conquer hunger, disease and illiteracy and to encourage respect for each other's rights and freedoms

» to be a centre for helping nations achieve these goals

The United Nations flag.

The design is a map of the world surrounded by a wreath consisting of crossed olive branches. The world map is centred on the North Pole and extends to 60 degrees south latitude: this projection allows for all countries to be displayed with none at the centre, representing the equality of all nations. The olive branches symbolize peace.

The original colours were gold on a field of smoke-blue with all water areas in white.

FLAG

The official flag of the United Nations was adopted on 20 October 1947. It consists of the official emblem of the United Nations in white on a blue background. The emblem is one half the height of the flag and entirely centred.

STRUCTURE OF THE ORGANIZATION

The work of the United Nations is carried out almost all over the world by six principal organs:

» General Assembly

» Security Council

» Economic and Social Council

» Trusteeship Council

» International Court of Justice

» Secretariat

All these organs are based at United Nations Headquarters in New York, except for the International Court of Justice, which is located at The Hague, Netherlands.

There are 15 specialized agencies that coordinate their work with the United Nations. In addition, there are 24 UN programmes, funds, institutes and other bodies with responsibilities in specific fields. All in all, the United Nations family of organizations focuses on areas as diverse as health, food and agriculture, telecommunications, tourism, labour, postal services, the environment, civil aviation, children, atomic energy, cultural preservation, science, refugees, intellectual property, gender equality, drugs, crime and terrorism, human settlements, maritime transport and weather. All these various bodies work together with the United Nations Secretariat and compose the United Nations System.

The United Nations Entity for Gender Equality and the Empowerment of Women, known as UN-Women, created in 2010, is the latest addition to the United Nations family of organizations. It replaces four separate entities devoted to women's issues.

You will find more information on the United Nations organs and the family of organizations in chapter two.

UNITED NATIONS HEADQUARTERS

The United Nations Headquarters in New York is an international zone. This means that the land on which the United Nations sits does not belong to just the United States, the host country, but to all the Members. The United Nations has its own flag and its own security officers who guard the area. It also has its own post office and issues its own stamps. These stamps can be used only from United Nations Headquarters or from United Nations offices in Vienna and Geneva. The compound has its own onsite bookshop which specializes in UN affairs and related topics.

THE BUILDING THAT ROSE FROM A RUNDOWN AREA

At its first meeting in London in 1946, the United Nations General Assembly decided to locate the United Nations Headquarters in the United States. Philadelphia, Boston, Chicago, San Francisco, etc. were all considered to host the United Nations Headquarters. What eventually persuaded the General Assembly to settle on the present site was a last-minute gift of $8.5 million from John D. Rockefeller, Jr. Later, New York City offered additional property as a gift.

In the mid-1940s, the site chosen for the United Nations Headquarters was a rundown area of slaughterhouses, a railroad garage and other commercial buildings.

On 24 October 1949, United Nations Secretary-General Trygve Lie laid the cornerstone of the 39-storey building. On 21 August 1950, the Secretariat's staff began moving into their new offices. The United Nations Headquarters buildings in New York were designed by an international team of 11 architects, including Oscar Niemeyer (Brazil) and Le Corbusier (Switzerland/France).

The United Nations Headquarters in New York today.

MEMBERSHIP AND BUDGET

The United Nations currently has four completely distinct budget lines:

» The regular budget, for core functions at Headquarters in New York, major regional offices at Geneva, Nairobi and Vienna and a range of field offices situated in all continents.

» The peacekeeping budget, to cover the cost of peacekeeping operations, often in war-torn zones, around the world.

» The budget for the International Criminal Tribunal for Rwanda, situated in Arusha, Tanzania, and the International Criminal Tribunal for the Former Yugoslavia, situated in The Hague, Netherlands.

» An approved budget of $1.9 billion allocated towards a renovation project of the United Nations Headquarters—the Capital Master Plan (CMP)—which is expected to be complete by 2014.

Payment to the United Nations for all types of budgets is compulsory. Members pay according to an agreed-upon scale of assessment. This scale, reviewed every three years, is based on a country's ability to pay, national income and population.

The specialized organizations that form part of the United Nations System have budgets separate from the four United Nations budgets described above. The bulk of their resources emanate from voluntary contributions by governments, individuals and institutions.

A GOOD VALUE FOR THE MONEY

The regular budget for the United Nations is approved by the General Assembly for a two-year period. The budget approved for 2012-2013 is $5.15 billion, which pays for United Nations activities, staff and basic infrastructure.

For peacekeeping, the budget for the year from 1 July 2011 to 30 June 2012 was roughly $7 billion. In comparison, in 2010, the world spent around $1.63 trillion on military expenditures. One year of global military spending could pay the United Nations peacekeeping budget for over 232 years. Peace is far cheaper than war and a good value for the money.

FOCUS ON

FUNDING THE UNITED NATIONS[1]

Most of the work of the United Nations is funded by contributions from all Member States. Additional funds come from commercial activities (guided tours, the sale of publications, databases, apps, etc.) or from a public or private entity that donates money to a trust fund managed by the United Nations for the purpose of a special project or programme.

The following Member States were the largest contributors to the 2012 United Nations regular budget:

Member States	Contributions (in millions of US dollars)	Contributions (percentage of the budget)
United States of America	568,750,776	22.0%
Japan	323,929,419	12.5%
Germany	207,283,806	8.0%
United Kingdom of Great Britain and Northern Ireland	170,728,642	6.6%
France	158,293,682	6.1%
Italy	129,235,688	5.0%
Canada	82,908,352	3.2%
China	82,443,010	3.2%
Spain	82,132,783	3.2%
Mexico	60,908,038	2.4%
Republic of Korea	58,426,216	2.3%
Australia	49,972,511	1.9%
Netherlands	47,956,031	1.9%
Brazil	41,648,068	1.6%
Russian Federation	41,415,397	1.6%

---

[1] Source: *www.un.org/en/ga*

BECOMING A MEMBER OF THE UNITED NATIONS

Membership, in accordance with the Charter of the United Nations, "is open to all peace-loving States that accept the obligations contained in the United Nations Charter and, in the judgment of the Organization, are able to carry out these obligations". States are admitted by decision of the General Assembly upon the recommendation of the Security Council.

In brief, the procedure is as follows:

» The requesting country or entity submits an application to the Secretary-General and a letter formally stating that it accepts the obligations under the Charter.

» The Security Council considers the application. Any recommendation for admission must receive affirmative votes from 9 of the 15 members of the Council, provided that none of its five permanent members—China, France, the Russian Federation, the United Kingdom and the United States of America—has voted against the application.

» If the Council recommends admission, the recommendation is presented to the General Assembly for consideration. A two-thirds majority vote is necessary in the Assembly for admission of a new State.

» Membership becomes effective on the day the resolution for admission is adopted.

PERMANENT OBSERVERS

Non-Member States of the United Nations, which are members of one or more specialized agencies, can apply for the status of Permanent Observer. The status of a Permanent Observer is based purely on practice; there are no provisions for it in the United Nations Charter. The practice dates from 1946, when the Secretary-General accepted the designation of neutral Switzerland as a Permanent Observer to

 DID YOU KNOW?

MEMBERSHIP GREW FROM 51 STATES IN 1945 TO 193 IN 2012

South Sudan officially broke away from Sudan on 9 July 2011. Its independence is the result of the January 2011 referendum held under the terms of the 2005 Comprehensive Peace Agreement (CPA) that ended the decades-long civil war between the North and the South. On 13 July 2011, the Security Council adopted a resolution to recommend to the General Assembly that the Republic of South Sudan be admitted to membership in the United Nations. On 17 July 2011, the General Assembly admitted the Republic of South Sudan as the 193rd member of the United Nations, welcoming the newly independent country to the world community.

the United Nations. Switzerland became a Member State in 2002. By 2012, the Holy See (Vatican City) was the sole sovereign State with Permanent Observer status and Palestine was the sole entity with such status.

Permanent Observers have free access to most meetings and relevant documentation. Many regional and international organizations are also observers of the work and annual sessions of the General Assembly.

OFFICIAL LANGUAGES

The official languages used at the United Nations are Arabic, Chinese, English, French, Russian and Spanish. The working languages at the United Nations Secretariat are English and French.

During meetings, delegates may speak in any of the official languages, and the speech is interpreted simultaneously in the other official languages. Most United Nations documents are also issued in all six official languages.

At times, a delegate may choose to make a statement using a non-official language. In such cases, the delegation must provide either an interpretation or a written text of the statement in one of the official languages.

South Sudan's national flag (fourth from left) flies at UN Headquarters following the admission of the country as the 193rd Member State.

TEST YOUR KNOWLEDGE

1. Who first mentioned the idea of an organization to safeguard a community of nations living in peace?

2. What is the name of the first-ever international organization whose aim was to maintain world peace?

3. What was the League of Nations?

4. When and why was the League of Nations dissolved?

5. In what year was the United Nations founded?

6. Who coined the phrase "United Nations"?

7. In which European capital city did the UN General Assembly first meet?

8. When was the Declaration by United Nations signed?

9. Only 50 countries were represented at the San Francisco Conference, so how did the United Nations come to have 51 original Member States?

10. Which country was the first to sign the United Nations Charter and why?

11. What is the list of rules and regulations of the United Nations called?

12. What are the four purposes of the United Nations?

13. What surrounds the world map on the United Nations flag, and what does it symbolize?

14. Why was New York City chosen as the site of the United Nations Headquarters?

15. Name three of the top contributors to the United Nations regular budget.

16. How many Member States does the United Nations have today?

17. Has any country ever left the United Nations?

18. Can an individual person become a Member of the United Nations?

19. How many principal organs does the United Nations have?

20. What are the official languages of the United Nations?

CHAPTER 2

THE UNITED NATIONS FAMILY

QUICK FACTS
ABOUT THE UNITED NATIONS FAMILY

The **work of the United Nations** is carried out by six main bodies and a family of organizations including 15 agencies, 24 programmes and other specialized entities.

———————————

In 2010, the United Nations Children's Fund (UNICEF) bought 2.5 billion doses of **vaccines** and distributed them in 99 countries, reaching 58 per cent of the world's children.

———————————

The Office of the United Nations High Commissioner for Refugees (UNHCR) provides aid and protection to more than 36 million **refugees and displaced persons** worldwide.

———————————

The United Nations System is involved in creating **technical standards** in telecommunications, civil aviation, shipping and postal services, making international transactions possible.

———————————

The United Nations and its specialized agency the World Health Organization (WHO) campaign for universal **immunization against childhood diseases**. As a result, smallpox has been eradicated and cases of polio have been reduced by 99 per cent.

———————————

The World Food Programme, the United Nations frontline food aid organization, ships an average of 3.7 million tons of food annually, reaching out in 2011 to some 90 million people in 73 countries.

———————————

During the past decade, the World Bank, through the International Development Association (IDA), helped save at least 13 million lives. IDA financing immunized 310 million children and provided **access to water and sanitation** for 177 million people.

———————————

The United Nations Educational, Scientific and Cultural Organization (UNESCO) had already placed **936 historical sites** on its World Heritage List by the end of 2011. The world's heritage is our legacy from the past, what we live with today and what we pass on to future generations.

———————————

CHAPTER 2
THE UNITED NATIONS FAMILY

PRINCIPAL ORGANS OF THE UNITED NATIONS

The Charter establishes six principal organs of the United Nations. This is a summary of their composition and functions.

GENERAL ASSEMBLY

All members of the United Nations (currently 193 States) are represented in the General Assembly. Each nation, rich or poor, large or small, has one vote:

» China, which has over a billion people, gets one vote; so does Nauru, with its 13,000 inhabitants.

» The largest country in the world, the Russian Federation, has one vote, just like the Principality of Monaco, which is roughly the size of New York City's Central Park.

A Member State can lose its vote if it fails to pay its dues and owes the Organization an amount equal to or exceeding the contributions due for two preceding years. An exception is allowed if the Member State can show that conditions beyond its control contributed to this inability to pay.

In the General Assembly, decisions on such issues as international peace and security, admission of new Member States and the United Nations budget are decided by a two-thirds majority. Other matters require only a simple majority. In recent years, a special effort has been made to reach decisions through consensus, rather than by taking a formal vote.

The General Assembly's regular session begins on Tuesday in the third week of September and continues throughout the year. At the beginning of each regular session, the Assembly holds a general debate at which Heads of State or Government and others present views on a wide-ranging agenda of issues of concern to the international community, from war and terrorism to disease and poverty.

Each year, the General Assembly elects a President who presides over the meetings. To ensure equitable geographical representation, the presidency rotates among five groups of countries:

- » African States
- » Asian States
- » Eastern European States
- » Latin American and Caribbean States
- » Western European and other States

Functions
The General Assembly is the principal organ that

- » discusses and makes recommendations on any subject, except those being considered at the same time by the Security Council
- » discusses questions related to military conflicts and the arms race
- » discusses ways and means to improve the status of children, youths, women and others
- » discusses issues related to sustainable development and human rights
- » decides how much each Member State should pay to the United Nations and how this money is spent

Main Committees
Because of the overwhelming number of questions it is called upon to consider, the General Assembly allocates items among its six Main Committees and other subsidiary organs. The Committees and organs discuss the issues, seeking as much as possible to harmonize the various positions different countries may have, and then present to a plenary (full) meeting of the Assembly draft resolutions and decisions for consideration.

The six Main Committees are:

- » the First Committee, which deals with issues of disarmament and international security

The General Assembly Hall accommodates all delegations. Each delegation has six seats, and there is a gallery for the media and the public, making a total of 1,898 seats.

» the Second Committee, which specializes in economic and financial questions

» the Third Committee, which focuses on social, humanitarian and cultural topics

» the Fourth Committee, which addresses special political issues and questions relating to decolonization

» the Fifth Committee, which works on administrative and budgetary questions

» the Sixth Committee, which reviews legal issues

Examples of actions taken by the General Assembly

» In September 2000, the General Assembly adopted the United Nations Millennium Declaration, a global commitment to reduce extreme poverty, with a deadline of 2015, which has become known as the Millennium Development Goals.

» In 2006, United Nations Member States agreed on a process of reforming the work of the General Assembly to speed up the decision-making process, streamline the agenda and strengthen the role and authority of the General Assembly President.

» In 2006, the General Assembly approved the establishment of a new, strengthened Human Rights Council to replace the United Nations Human Rights Commission. The Council, which was inaugurated on 19 June 2006 in Geneva, has a higher status in the United Nations System as a subsidiary body of the General Assembly.

» In July 2010, the General Assembly created UN-Women, a historic step towards the realization of the Organization's goals on gender equality and the empowerment of women. UN-Women brings together the resources and mandates of four previously distinct UN entities for greater impact. Empowering women sparks progress in education, health, productivity and the economy, and therefore boosts a country's level of development.

» In September 2010, the General Assembly created a new Global Strategy for Women's and Children's Health. The initiative aims to save the lives of more than 16 million women and children, help prevent 33 million unwanted pregnancies, protect 120 million children from pneumonia and 88 million children from stunting due to malnutrition.

» In December 2010, the General Assembly declared 2011-2020 the United Nations Decade on Biodiversity. Protecting biodiversity is in our self-interest. Biological resources are the pillars upon which we build civilizations. The loss of biodiversity threatens our food supplies, our opportunities for recreation and tourism and our sources of wood, medicines and energy. It also interferes with essential ecological functions.

» In September 2011, recognizing that non-communicable diseases constitute one of the major challenges for development in the twenty-first century, the General Assembly called a high-level meeting. The world leaders gathered in New York agreed to adopt, before the end of 2012, targets to combat heart disease, cancer, diabetes and lung disease, and to devise policies that would cut smoking and slash the high salt, sugar and fat content in foods that cause obesity, injury and death.

The Security Council chamber, a gift from Norway, was designed by Norwegian artist Arnstein Arneberg. A large mural by Per Krohg (Norway), symbolizing the promise of future peace and individual freedom, covers most of the east wall.

SECURITY COUNCIL

While the General Assembly can discuss any world concern, the Security Council is primarily responsible for questions of peace and security.

Functions

The Security Council is the principal organ that

» investigates any dispute or situation that might lead to international conflict

» recommends methods and terms of settlement

» recommends actions against any threat or act of aggression

» recommends to the General Assembly who should be appointed as Secretary-General of the United Nations

Membership

The Security Council has 15 members. Five are permanent members: China, France, the Russian Federation, the United Kingdom and the United States. The other 10 non-permanent members are elected by the General Assembly for two-year terms and are chosen on the basis of geographical representation.

FIVE COUNTRIES HAVE THE RIGHT TO VETO

At the end of the Second World War, China, France, the Soviet Union (which was succeeded in 1990 by the Russian Federation), the United Kingdom and the United States played key roles in the establishment of the United Nations. The creators of the United Nations Charter thought that these five countries would continue to play important roles in the maintenance of international peace and security. So the "big five" were given a special voting power unofficially known as the "right to veto." The drafters agreed that if any one of the "big five" cast a negative vote in the 15-member Security Council, the resolution or decision would not be approved.

Some Member States have been advocating for changes in the membership of the Security Council. They want to increase the number of permanent members to include more of the world's largest countries, and they argue that African issues represent 70 per cent of the Security Council's work, yet the continent still lacks permanent representation.

Meetings

The Security Council, unlike the General Assembly, does not hold regular meetings. Instead, it can be called to meet at any given time and at very short notice. Members take turns at being President of the Security Council for a month at a time. They serve in the English-language alphabetical order of the names of the Member States they represent.

To pass a resolution in the Security Council, 9 out of the 15 members must vote "yes"; however, if any of the five permanent members votes "no"—such a vote is often referred to as a veto—the resolution does not pass.

Examples of actions taken by the Security Council

» The Council established two international criminal tribunals to prosecute those responsible for war crimes and crimes against humanity in the former Yugoslavia and in Rwanda during the 1990s.

» Following the terrorist attacks on the United States on 11 September 2001, the Council established its Counter-Terrorism Committee to help States increase their capability to fight terrorism.

» In July 2007, the Council voted unanimously to deploy a 26,000-strong joint United Nations-African Union Mission in Darfur (UNAMID) in an attempt to quell the violence in Sudan's western Darfur region, where fighting between pro-government militias and rebel guerrillas had killed more than 250,000 people since 2003.

» On 9 June 2010, because of Iran's lack of compliance with previous resolutions ensuring the peaceful nature of its nuclear programme, the Security Council imposed more sanctions on the country, expanding an arms embargo and tightening restrictions on financial and shipping enterprises related to nuclear "proliferation-sensitive activities".

» On 17 March 2011, the Council adopted Resolution 1973, imposing a ban on all flights in Libya's airspace (no-fly zone) and tightening sanctions on the regime of Colonel Muammar Gaddafi and its armed supporters. The goal was to prevent further deadly attacks on civilians during the civil war in that country.

» In July 2011, following the declaration of independence of South Sudan, the Council established a new mission, the United Nations Mission in the Republic of South Sudan (UNMISS), in an attempt to foster peace and security and to help create favourable conditions for development in the new country.

ECONOMIC AND SOCIAL COUNCIL (ECOSOC)

The Economic and Social Council (ECOSOC) is the forum for discussion of economic questions, such as trade, transport and economic development, and social issues, such as poverty and better livelihoods. It also helps countries reach agreements on how to improve education and health conditions and how to promote respect for, and observance of, universal human rights and freedoms of people everywhere.

Functions

The ECOSOC is the principal organ that

» promotes higher standards of living, full employment, and economic and social progress

» identifies solutions to international economic, social and health problems

» facilitates international cultural and educational cooperation

» encourages universal respect for human rights and fundamental freedoms

The ECOSOC has the power to make or initiate studies and reports on these issues. It is also involved in the preparation and organization of major international conferences in the economic, social and related fields and is involved in the practical follow-ups to these conferences.

Membership
The ECOSOC has 54 members that serve for three-year terms. Voting in the Council is by simple majority; each member has one vote.

Each year, the ECOSOC holds several short sessions focused on the planning of its own work, often including representatives of civil society. The Council also holds an annual four-week "substantive" session in July to discuss matters of major or practical importance to all concerned countries, alternating the venue between Geneva and New York.

Subsidiary bodies
The ECOSOC has a variety of commissions to administer the wide range of issues that fall within its purview, including:

»   the Commission on Narcotic Drugs

»   the Commission for Social Development

»   the Commission on Population and Development

»   the Statistical Commission

»   the Commission on Crime Prevention and Criminal Justice

»   the Commission on Sustainable Development

»   the Commission on Science and Technology for Development

»   the United Nations Forum on Forests

The Council also directs five regional commissions:

»   the Economic Commission for Africa (ECA)

»   the Economic Commission for Europe (ECE), which also covers the countries of North America and the former USSR

»   the Economic Commission for Latin America and the Caribbean (ECLAC)

»   the Economic and Social Commission for Asia and the Pacific (ESCAP)

»   the Economic and Social Commission for Western Asia (ESCWA), which covers the Arab countries located in Asia, plus Egypt and Sudan

TRUSTEESHIP COUNCIL

In 1945, when the United Nations was established, 11 non-self-governing territories (mostly in Africa and the Pacific Ocean) were placed under international supervision. The major goals of the trusteeship system were to promote the advancement of the inhabitants of such Trust Territories and their progression towards self-government or independence.

Membership

The Trusteeship Council is composed of the permanent members of the Security Council (China, France, the Russian Federation, the United Kingdom and the United States). Each member has one vote, and decisions are made by a simple majority.

Meetings

Since the last Trust Territory—Palau, formerly administered by the United States—achieved self-government in 1994 and became a Member State of the United Nations, the Council formally suspended operations after nearly half a century. It will meet again only as the need arises.

FOCUS ON

DECOLONIZATION

In 1945, half of the world's people lived in countries that were governed from outside. These countries, known as colonies, were controlled by a handful of major, mostly—but not only—European powers. Through the process known as decolonization, the United Nations has helped the colonies gain independence. The General Assembly, in 1960, adopted a declaration to urge the speedy independence of all colonies and peoples. The following year, it set up a Special Committee on Decolonization. As a result of the United Nations' efforts, more than 80 former colonies are now themselves members of the Organization.

Today, about one million people live in dependent territories. Many of the territories—for the most part small or isolated islands—wish to remain associated with their outside administering powers and have established autonomous local institutions to manage their own affairs. However, after the withdrawal of Spain as administering power in 1976, the question of the status of Western Sahara has yet to be resolved. This remains a focus of United Nations attention, with the United Nations Mission for the Referendum in Western Sahara (MINURSO) established in 1991. A referendum under discussion would invite the territory's inhabitants to decide if they desire full independence as a sovereign State or integration with Morocco.

INTERNATIONAL COURT OF JUSTICE

The International Court of Justice, also known as the World Court, was established by the Charter of the United Nations in 1945 and began its work in April 1946. The seat of the Court is at the Peace Palace in The Hague (Netherlands). Of the six principal organs of the United Nations, it is the only one not located in New York.

Functions

The Court is the principal organ that

> » settles legal disputes submitted by States in accordance with international law

> » gives advisory opinions on legal questions referred by authorized United Nations organs and specialized agencies

States bring disputes before the Court in search of impartial solutions to their differences with other countries. By achieving peaceful settlement on such questions as land frontiers, maritime boundaries and territorial sovereignty, the Court

After an international competition, French architect Louis Cordonnier won the design of the Peace Palace in The Hague, Netherlands. It has housed the International Court of Justice and its predecessors since 1913.

has often helped prevent the escalation of disputes into larger conflicts that could lead to loss of life.

All judgments passed by the Court are final and cannot be appealed.

Membership
The Court is composed of 15 judges elected by the General Assembly and the Security Council. No two judges can be from the same country, and it takes a majority of nine judges to make a decision. The Court is assisted by a Registry, its administrative organ.

Cases and advisory opinions
In its judgments, the Court has addressed international disputes involving economic rights, environmental protection, rights of passage, the use of force, interference in the internal affairs of States, diplomatic relations, hostage taking, the right of asylum and nationality.

Since 1946, the International Court of Justice has considered some 150 cases, issued numerous judgments on disputes brought to it by States and issued advisory opinions in response to requests by a range of United Nations organizations. The number of cases submitted to the Court has increased significantly since the 1970s, when it decided only one or two cases at any given time. At the beginning of 2012, there were 16 cases pending in the Court, including one under active consideration.

The Court's advisory opinions have dealt with, among other things, membership admission to the United Nations, reparation for injuries suffered in the service of the United Nations, the territorial status of Western Sahara and the legality of the threat or use of nuclear weapons.

SECRETARIAT

The Secretariat, headed by the Secretary-General, consists of staff representing nationalities from all over the world. They carry out the day-to-day work of the United Nations; their duties are as varied as the problems dealt with by the Organization. These range from administering peacekeeping operations to mediating international disputes to surveying social and economic trends. The Secretariat serves the other organs of the United Nations and is responsible for administering the programmes and policies laid down by them.

Functions

The Secretariat is the principal organ that

» administers peacekeeping operations, mediates international disputes and organizes humanitarian relief programmes

» surveys economic and social trends, prepares studies on human rights, sustainable development and other areas of concern, and publishes a variety of publications

» lays the groundwork for international agreements

» informs the world—the media, governments, non-governmental organizations, research and academic networks, schools and colleges and the general public—about the work of the United Nations

» assists in carrying out the decisions of the United Nations

» organizes international conferences on subjects of vital concern for humankind

» interprets speeches and translates documents into the six official languages of the United Nations

 MORE INFO

THE OFFICE OF THE HIGH COMMISSIONER FOR HUMAN RIGHTS IS PART OF THE SECRETARIAT

The Office of the United Nations High Commissioner for Human Rights (OHCHR) is not a United Nations agency but an integral part of the United Nations Secretariat. Headquartered in Geneva, it represents the world's commitment to universal ideals of human dignity. OHCHR works with all governments to help promote and implement human rights worldwide.

It provides assistance, such as expertise and technical training in the administration of justice, legislative reform and electoral process, to help implement international human rights standards on the ground.

OHCHR also assists other entities with the protection of human rights; helps all women, children and men realize their rights and legitimate aspirations; and speaks out in the face of human rights violations committed around the world by State and non-State actors. Unfortunately, there are still many human rights violations taking place today, which necessitate the independent and objective scrutiny of the United Nations.

Secretary-General

The Charter of the United Nations describes the Secretary-General as the chief administrative officer of the Organization, who shall act in this capacity and perform "functions as are entrusted" to him or her by the General Assembly, Security Council, Economic and Social Council and other United Nations organs.

The Secretary-General is assisted by staff from all countries—people referred to as "international civil servants." Unlike traditional diplomats, who represent a particular country and its interests, international civil servants work for all 193 Member States and take their orders not from governments but from the Secretary-General. They are independent from political and other forms of interference and place the interests of the Organization above their own.

? DID YOU KNOW?

THE SECRETARY-GENERAL DOES NOT ACT ALONE

The Secretary-General does not act without the support and approval of the United Nations Member States. Any course of action, whether it concerns sending peacekeeping troops to war-torn areas or helping a country rebuild after a war or a natural disaster, must be set by the Member States.

Role of the Secretary-General

The Secretary-General

» proposes issues to be discussed by the General Assembly or any other organ of the United Nations

» brings to the attention of the Security Council any problem that he or she feels may threaten world peace

» acts as a "referee" in disputes between Member States

» offers his or her "good offices"—steps taken publicly and in private, drawing upon the Secretary-General's independence, impartiality and integrity, as well as his or her prestige and the weight of the international community, to prevent international disputes from arising, escalating or spreading

 FOCUS ON

BAN KI-MOON, UNITED NATIONS SECRETARY-GENERAL

Ban Ki-moon is the eighth Secretary-General of the United Nations. His priorities are to mobilize world leaders around a set of new global challenges, from climate change and economic upheaval to pandemics and increasing pressures involving food, energy and water. He seeks to build bridges between Member States, give voice to the world's poorest and most vulnerable people and strengthen the Organization itself.

"I grew up in war", the Secretary-General has said, "and saw the United Nations help my country to recover and rebuild. That experience was a big part of what led me to pursue a career in public service. As Secretary-General, I am determined to see this Organization deliver tangible, meaningful results that advance peace, development and human rights." Mr. Ban took office on 1 January 2007.

Highlights of Mr. Ban's five-year action agenda for his second term (2012-2017) include:

» Promoting sustainable development by accelerating progress towards the Millennium Development Goals, addressing climate change issues and establishing a new sustainable development framework to be implemented after 2015.

» Enabling effective disaster prevention by supporting the development and implementation of national disaster risk reduction plans, prioritizing early warning and early action on preventing violent conflict, advancing a preventive approach to human rights and building resilience to economic and financial shocks.

» Building a safer and more secure world by strengthening partnerships for peacekeeping, establishing a more global, accountable and robust humanitarian system, revitalizing the global disarmament and non-proliferation of arms agenda, scaling up counter-terrorism efforts and addressing the threats of organized crime, piracy and drug trafficking.

» Supporting nations in transition by developing best practices and scaling up the United Nations capacity and support in key areas, advocating for and establishing accountability in all domains and deepening collaboration with international, regional and local partners.

» Working with and for women and young people by fighting to end violence against women, promoting women's political participation worldwide, ensuring the full participation of women in social and economic recovery and addressing the needs of the largest generation of young people the world has ever known.

Appointment of the Secretary-General

The Secretary-General is appointed for a period of five years by the General Assembly on the recommendation of the Security Council. There have been eight Secretaries-General since the United Nations was created. The appointment of the Secretary-General follows a regional rotation.

Former Secretaries-General

Those who have served as Secretary-General since the creation of the United Nations are:

» Trygve Lie (Norway): 1946-1952

» Dag Hammarskjöld (Sweden): 1953-1961

» U Thant (Burma): 1961-1971

» Kurt Waldheim (Austria): 1972-1981

» Javier Pérez de Cuéllar (Peru): 1982-1991

» Boutros Boutros-Ghali (Egypt): 1992-1996

» Kofi Annan (Ghana): 1997-2006

» Ban Ki-moon (South Korea): 2007-present

Trygve Lie   Dag Hammarskjöld   U Thant   Kurt Waldheim

Javier
Pérez de Cuéllar   Boutros
Boutros-Ghali   Kofi Annan   Ban Ki-moon

Four main offices

United Nations Headquarters in New York (UNHQ)

The United Nations Headquarters in New York (United States of America) by the numbers:

» 193 diplomatic delegations representing Member States, who send more than 5,000 people to New York each year for the annual sessions of the General Assembly

» 5,500 international staff members working in the Secretariat at New York

» One million visitors touring the Headquarters every year

» 2,000 journalists permanently accredited and nearly 3,500 present during major events and meetings

» More than 5,000 non-governmental organizations accredited to the United Nations, many of whom attend meetings at Headquarters

UN Headquarters in New York

UN Office at Geneva

UN Office at Nairobi

UN Office at Vienna

United Nations Office at Geneva (UNOG)

The United Nations Office at Geneva (Switzerland), the European regional headquarters, by the numbers:

» 184 diplomatic delegations representing Member States

» Around 8,500 staff members working for the United Nations and its specialized agencies, funds and programmes

» Close to 100,000 visitors touring the Palais des Nations every year

» 230 journalists permanently accredited

» Hundreds of non-governmental organizations accredited to the United Nations

» Approximately 9,960 meetings organized every year

The United Nations Office at Nairobi (UNON)

The United Nations Office at Nairobi (Kenya) serves as the global headquarters of the United Nations Environment Programme (UNEP) and the United Nations Programme for Human Settlements (UN-Habitat).

The United Nations Office at Nairobi by the numbers:

» 146 diplomatic delegations representing Member States

» 2,800 staff working at UNEP and UN-Habitat

» An array of diplomatic gatherings and peacebuilding initiatives

» Hundreds of people working for non-governmental organizations accredited to the United Nations

The United Nations Office at Vienna (UNOV)

The United Nations Office at Vienna (Austria) serves as headquarters for the International Atomic Energy Agency (IAEA), the United Nations Industrial Development Organization (UNIDO), the United Nations Office for Outer Space Affairs (UNOOSA) and the United Nations Office on Drugs and Crime (UNODC).

The United Nations Office at Vienna by the numbers:

» Dozens of diplomatic delegations representing Member States

» 4,000 employees working for the Vienna-based United Nations organizations

» Approximately 2,000 international conferences and meetings held annually

FOCUS ON

ABOUT THE UN REGIONAL OFFICES

The Palais des Nations

» The United Nations Office at Geneva building previously hosted the head-quarters of the League of Nations, the precursor to the United Nations. At the end of the Second World War, the League gave way to the United Nations, which inherited its physical assets, including an imposing architectural edifice referred to as the Palais des Nations (Palace of Nations).

The United Nations and Kenya

» The United Nations has promoted a variety of proposals to benefit the agricultural sector which employs nearly 80 per cent of all Kenyans. These include dry-lands farming and farmer field schools, as well as projects on water, electrification, refugees, drought relief, women's empowerment and HIV/AIDS.

» The United Nations has heavily invested in wildlife conservation, forest restoration and ecotourism, all of which provide unquantifiable economic benefits for local residents. It has supported thousands of community-based projects, touching hundreds of thousands of lives in Kenya.

"United Nations City" in Vienna

» The United Nations Office at Vienna, also known as the Vienna International Centre (VIC), opened its doors in August 1979. The six Y-shaped office towers were designed to let staff work in natural sunlight rather than artificial light in almost every office. Locally, the Vienna International Centre, which is situated on the outskirts of the Austrian capital, is often referred to as "United Nations City."

THE UNITED NATIONS: A FAMILY OF SPECIALIZED ENTITIES

There are 15 specialized agencies and 24 programmes, funds and other bodies with specific responsibilities all related to the United Nations. These programmes and bodies, together with the United Nations itself, compose the United Nations System.

The various entities belonging to the United Nations System are listed below by type of organization, and in alphabetical order within each type.

AGENCIES

Food and Agriculture Organization (FAO)
The Food and Agriculture Organization works to eradicate hunger and malnutrition and to raise levels of nutrition. It also assists Member States in the sustainable development of agriculture, forestry and fisheries, helping them move towards achieving food security. Combating hunger and malnutrition has important indirect effects on children, such as reducing child labour, allowing them to attend school and improving their health.

International Civil Aviation Organization (ICAO)
The International Civil Aviation Organization assures the safe, secure, orderly and sustainable development of international air transport while minimizing the adverse effect of global civil aviation on the environment. In an effort to combat child trafficking, it recommends that all countries require a separate passport for each child.

International Fund for Agricultural Development (IFAD)
The International Fund for Agricultural Development is dedicated to eradicating rural poverty in developing countries. Some 75 per cent of the world's poorest people—that is, one billion women, children and men—live in rural areas and depend on agriculture and related activities for their livelihoods. IFAD invests in agriculture and rural development projects that reach poor, marginalized and vulnerable people in rural areas and helps create the conditions they need to improve their lives.

International Labour Organization (ILO)
The International Labour Organization formulates policies and programmes to promote the basic human rights of workers, improve working and living conditions and enhance employment opportunities. It also leads efforts to eradicate child labour worldwide.

International Maritime Organization (IMO)

The International Maritime Organization is responsible for improving the safety and security of international shipping and for preventing marine pollution from ships. It is also involved in legal matters such as liability and compensation issues and the facilitation of international maritime traffic.

International Monetary Fund (IMF)

The International Monetary Fund promotes the stability of the global monetary and financial system. It advises on key economic policies, provides temporary financial assistance and training, promotes growth and alleviates poverty.

International Telecommunications Union (ITU)

The International Telecommunications Union is committed to connecting the world. The global international telecommunications network is one of the largest and most sophisticated engineering feats ever accomplished, and ITU is at its very heart. ITU negotiates agreements on technologies, services and allocation of global resources like radio-frequency spectrum and satellite orbital positions, creating a seamless global communications system that is robust, reliable and constantly evolving.

United Nations Educational, Scientific and Cultural Organization (UNESCO)

The United Nations Educational, Scientific and Cultural Organization promotes international cooperation and facilitates the exchange of information in the fields of education, science, culture and communications. It works to safeguard the world's cultural heritage. It aims to empower, educate and inspire young people, reaching out to them, responding to their expectations and ideas, and fostering useful and long-lasting skills.

United Nations Industrial Development Organization (UNIDO)

The United Nations Industrial Development Organization promotes and accelerates sustainable industrial growth in developing countries and economies in transition. It aims to give each country an opportunity to create a flourishing productive sector, increase its participation in international trade and safeguard its environment.

Universal Postal Union (UPU)

The Universal Postal Union sets the rules for international mail exchanges. It makes recommendations to stimulate growth in mail, parcel and financial-services and to improve the quality of service for customers. It also provides technical assistance where needed.

World Bank

The World Bank aims to overcome poverty, enhance economic growth while caring for the environment and create individual opportunities and hope. To this end, it provides low-interest loans, interest-free credits and grants to developing countries to be invested in education, health, public administration, infrastructure, financial and private-sector development, agriculture and environmental and natural resource management.

World Health Organization (WHO)

The World Health Organization is responsible for providing leadership on global health matters, shaping the health research agenda and setting norms and standards. Today, health is a shared responsibility, involving equitable access to essential care and collective defence against transboundary epidemic threats. Special emphasis is given to children's health, since they are more vulnerable to malnutrition and infectious diseases, many of which are preventable and treatable.

World Intellectual Property Organization (WIPO)

The World Intellectual Property Organization ensures that the rights of creators and owners of intellectual property—people such as musicians, writers, scientists and inventors—are protected worldwide and that creators are, therefore, recognized and rewarded for their ingenuity and creativity.

World Meteorological Organization (WMO)

The World Meteorological Organization coordinates global scientific research and data on the state and behaviour of the Earth's atmosphere, its interaction with the oceans, the climate it produces and the resulting distribution of water resources. WMO also provides vital information for early warnings of weather-, climate- and water-related phenomena, which cause nearly three quarters of all natural disasters, so as to save lives and minimize damage to property.

World Tourism Organization (UNWTO)

The World Tourism Organization promotes the development of responsible, environmentally and socially friendly and universally accessible tourism. Tourism alone represents 5 per cent of the total economic activity and 6 to 7 per cent of the overall number of jobs worldwide. UNWTO is engaged in a global campaign to protect children from all forms of exploitation in tourism, including sexual exploitation, child labour and trafficking.

FUNDS AND PROGRAMMES

United Nations Children's Fund (UNICEF)

The United Nations Children's Fund is the main United Nations organization defending, promoting and protecting children's rights. It focuses especially on the world's most disadvantaged children. On the ground, UNICEF promotes education for all boys and girls, immunizes against common childhood diseases and provides other health services, water and nutrition to children and adolescents.

United Nations Conference on Trade and Development (UNCTAD)

The United Nations Conference on Trade and Development promotes the integration of developing countries into the world economy. It helps shape debates and thinking on development and ensures that the policies of different countries and international action are mutually supportive in bringing about sustainable development.

United Nations Development Programme (UNDP)

The United Nations Development Programme is a global development network advocating for change and connecting countries to knowledge, experience and resources in order to help people build a better life. UNDP is on the ground in 166 countries, working with local inhabitants to find their own solutions to global and national development challenges.

UN-Women, United Nations Entity for Gender Equality and the Empowerment of Women

UN-Women, the United Nations Entity for Gender Equality and the Empowerment of Women seeks to eliminate discrimination against women and girls, to empower women and to achieve gender equality worldwide. In particular, UN-Women aims to uphold the human rights of girls, protecting them from all forms of violence and abuse and ensuring their access to health services and education.

United Nations Environment Programme (UNEP)

The United Nations Environment Programme provides leadership and encourages partnership in caring for the environment. It supports environmental monitoring, assessment and early warning of new dangers around the world.

Office of the United Nations High Commissioner for Refugees (UNHCR)

The Office of the United Nations High Commissioner for Refugees provides legal protection for refugees and seeks long-lasting solutions to their problems, by helping them either return voluntarily to their homes or settle in other countries. Nearly 50 per cent of the refugees worldwide are children. The UNHCR aims to uphold their rights, seeking to reunite them with their families and caregivers; protecting them from sexual exploitation, abuse, violence and military recruitment; and offering them education and training.

United Nations Human Settlements Programme (UN-Habitat)

The United Nations Human Settlements Programme promotes socially and environmentally sustainable towns and cities with the goal of ensuring adequate shelter for all.

United Nations Office on Drugs and Crime (UNODC)

The United Nations Office on Drugs and Crime focuses on stopping organized crime and trafficking, building criminal justice systems, preventing illicit drug use and the spread of HIV among drug users and other vulnerable groups, ending corruption and preventing terrorism. Monitoring drug and crime trends and threats, UNODC provides data that can help define drug and crime control priorities and help countries tackle these problems.

United Nations Population Fund (UNFPA)

The United Nations Population Fund promotes the right of women, men and children to enjoy a healthy life. UNFPA supports countries in using population data to determine policies and programmes that help reduce poverty and ensure every pregnancy is wanted, every birth is safe and every girl and woman is treated with dignity and respect.

United Nations Relief and Works Agency for Palestine Refugees in the Near East (UNRWA)

The United Nations Relief and Works Agency for Palestine Refugees in the Near East provides assistance, protection and advocacy for registered Palestine refugees. UNRWA offers education, health care, relief and social services, camp infrastructure and improvement, community support, microfinance and emergency response, including in times of armed conflict.

World Food Programme (WFP)

The World Food Programme combats global hunger, which afflicts one out of every seven people on Earth. In emergencies, WFP is on the frontline, delivering food to save the lives of victims of war, civil conflict and natural disaster. After an emergency has passed, WFP uses food to help communities rebuild their shattered lives. Thanks to the school meals programmes, WFP directly affects the lives of millions of children, providing them with vital nourishment that in turn improves their health and boosts their attendance in school.

RESEARCH AND TRAINING INSTITUTES

United Nations Institute for Disarmament Research (UNIDIR)

The United Nations Institute for Disarmament Research promotes research, creative thinking and dialogue on the disarmament and security challenges of today and tomorrow. UNIDIR deals with topics as diverse as nuclear materials, control of small arms ammunition, the security of refugee camps, disarmament as humanitarian action, peacekeeping and remote sensing technologies in the service of peace and disarmament, among other subjects.

United Nations Institute for Training and Research (UNITAR)

The United Nations Institute for Training and Research carries out research and training activities and develops pedagogical materials. Often working with other academic institutions, it offers instruction in the fields of peace and security, social and economic development, environment, multilateral diplomacy and international cooperation.

United Nations Interregional Crime and Justice Research Institute (UNICRI)

The United Nations Interregional Crime and Justice Research Institute tackles the threat of crime to peace, development and political stability. Its goals are to advance an understanding of crime-related problems, to foster fair and efficient criminal justice systems, including juvenile justice, to support the respect of international instruments of justice and other standards and to facilitate international law enforcement cooperation and judicial assistance.

United Nations Research Institute for Social Development (UNRISD)

The mission of the United Nations Research Institute for Social Development is to generate knowledge and articulate policy alternatives on contemporary development issues, thereby contributing to the broader goals of the UN system of reducing poverty and inequality, advancing well-being and rights, and creating more democratic and just societies. UNRISD was established as an autonomous space within the UN system for the conduct of policy-relevant, cutting-edge research on social development that is pertinent to the work of the United Nations Secretariat; regional commissions and specialized agencies; and national institutions.

United Nations System Staff College (UNSSC)

The United Nations System Staff College runs courses for United Nations personnel, assisting the staff of United Nations organizations in developing the skills and competencies needed to meet today's global challenges.

United Nations University (UNU)

The United Nations University contributes to the advancement of knowledge in fields relevant to the United Nations and to the application of that knowledge in formulating sound principles, policies, strategies and programmes for action. UNU activities are focused on five interlinked, interdependent thematic clusters: peace, security and human rights; human and socio-economic development and good governance; global health, population and sustainable livelihoods; global change and sustainable development; and science, technology, innovation and society.

OTHER ENTITIES

Joint United Nations Programme on HIV/AIDS (UNAIDS)

The Joint United Nations Programme on HIV/AIDS is an innovative partnership that leads and inspires the world in achieving complete access for all to HIV prevention, treatment, care and support. The objective is zero new HIV infections, zero discrimination and zero AIDS-related deaths. This requires long-term investment, and the strategy of UNAIDS is to bolster prevention, treatment, care and support, as well as advance human rights and gender equality.

United Nations International Strategy for Disaster Reduction (UNISDR)

The United Nations International Strategy for Disaster Reduction is the secretariat of the strategic framework for disaster reduction adopted by United Nations Member States in 2000. UNISDR guides and coordinates the efforts of a range of partners to achieve a large reduction in disaster losses. It aims to build resilient nations and communities, an essential condition for sustainable development.

UNOPS United Nations Office for Project Services (UNOPS)

The United Nations Office for Project Services aims to expand the capacity of the United Nations System and its partners to implement peacebuilding, humanitarian and development operations that matter for people in need. Core services include project, human resources and financial management, as well as the procurement of material and other services.

RELATED ORGANIZATIONS

International Atomic Energy Agency (IAEA)

The International Atomic Energy Agency serves as the global focal point for nuclear cooperation. It assists countries in planning for and using nuclear science and technology for peaceful purposes, such as the generation of electricity, and it develops nuclear safety standards. IAEA also uses a system of inspections to ensure that States comply with their commitment to use nuclear material and facilities only for peaceful purposes.

Organization for the Prohibition of Chemical Weapons (OPCW)

The Organization for the Prohibition of Chemical Weapons is dedicated to the implementation of the Convention on the Prohibition of the Development, Production, Stockpiling and Use of Chemical Weapons and on their Destruction (usually referred to as the Chemical Weapons Convention). The main obligation under the Convention is the prohibition of use and production of chemical weapons, as well as the destruction of all chemical weapons. The destruction activities are verified by the OPCW which also verifies that toxic chemicals that States produce are not intended for use as weapons of mass destruction.

Preparatory Commission for the Comprehensive Nuclear-Test-Ban Treaty Organization (CTBTO)

The Preparatory Commission for the Comprehensive Nuclear-Test-Ban Treaty Organization promotes the Comprehensive Nuclear-Test-Ban Treaty, which prohibits nuclear explosions by anyone anywhere on the Earth's surface, in the atmosphere, underwater or underground. CTBTO also has a monitoring system set up around the world to make sure that no nuclear explosion goes undetected. The Treaty will enter into force when the required number of countries ratifies it.

World Trade Organization (WTO)

The World Trade Organization is a forum for governments to negotiate trade agreements and settle trade disputes. It operates a system of trade rules. WTO is the place where Member States try to sort out the trade problems they face with each other.

MESSENGERS OF PEACE AND GOODWILL AMBASSADORS

The United Nations Messengers of Peace and Goodwill Ambassadors are distinguished and carefully selected individuals who volunteer to help focus worldwide attention on the work of the United Nations through public appearances, contact with the international media and humanitarian work.

From the earliest days of the United Nations, actors, artists, football and tennis players, gymnasts, designers, composers, ballet dancers, astronauts, entrepreneurs, scientists, writers, singers, philosophers, fashion models and members of governments and royal families—talented and compassionate women and men from around the world—have lent their names, public recognition and fame in support of the United Nations' work for a better world.

The system of United Nations Goodwill Ambassadors and Honorary Ambassadors began in 1954, when UNICEF appointed American actor Danny Kaye its first Goodwill Ambassador. In 1998, a new, related programme was added with the creation of Messengers of Peace.

While Goodwill and Honorary Ambassadors mainly promote the work of the United Nations agencies they represent, the Messengers of Peace champion the work of the United Nations in general and are appointed directly by the Secretary-General.

The Messengers of Peace are initially chosen for a period of two years, although some of the current 12 Messengers have served for more than 10 years.

TEST YOUR KNOWLEDGE

1. How many principal organs does the United Nations have, and what are they?

2. What is the main judicial organ of the United Nations?

3. What matters does the General Assembly discuss and/or make suggestions on?

4. True or false: China has more votes in the General Assembly than Monaco because its population is larger.

5. How many members does the Security Council have?

6. What is a "veto", and who has veto power?

7. What is the concern of the ECOSOC?

8. Where is the International Court of Justice located?

9. How many judges does the International Court of Justice have?

10. Can several judges of the International Court of Justice come from the same country?

11. Which country was the last Trust Territory to achieve self-government thanks to the Trusteeship Council?

12. Who are the people who work in the Secretariat and what are they called?

13. Name two Secretaries-General.

14. Who was Dag Hammarskjöld?

15. Apart from the Headquarters in New York, where are the other main offices of the United Nations located?

16. What are the main responsibilities of the Office of the High Commissioner for Human Rights?

17. What does UNICEF stand for?

18. Which United Nations organization advocates for every person, including every child, regardless of nationality, to carry his or her own passport, and why?

19. What is the name of the United Nations agency that deals with epidemics?

20. What do the Messengers of Peace and Goodwill Ambassadors do?

CHAPTER 3

ECONOMIC AND
SOCIAL DEVELOPMENT

QUICK FACTS
ON ECONOMIC AND SOCIAL DEVELOPMENT

By 2015, the **global poverty rate** is expected to fall below 15 per cent, well under the 23 per cent target set by the Millennium Development Goals, in spite of significant setbacks after the worldwide 2008-2009 financial crisis and ensuing great recession.

___

The number of **deaths of children** under the age of five declined from 12.4 million in 1990 to 8.1 million in 2009; however, this still means that, in the next minute, 15 children under the age of five will die around the world.

___

An estimated 1.1 billion people in urban areas and 723 million people in rural areas gained access to an **improved drinking water** source between 1990 and 2008; however, over 2.6 billion people still lack access to flush toilets or other forms of **improved sanitation**.

___

New **HIV infections** are declining steadily, led by a big decrease in sub-Saharan Africa. In 2009, an estimated 2.6 million people were infected with HIV—a drop of 21 per cent since 1997, when new infections peaked.

___

Progress in ameliorating **slum conditions** has not been sufficient to offset the growth of informal settlements throughout the developing world. In developing regions, the number of urban residents living in slum conditions is now estimated at 828 million, compared to 657 million in 1990 and 767 million in 2000.

___

Nearly every minute, a child is born with HIV. Giving pregnant women living with HIV access to **antiretroviral** prevention and treatment reduces the risk of a child being born with the virus to less than 5 per cent—and keeps their mothers alive to raise them.

___

Up to 3.6 million deaths could be avoided each year in 58 developing countries if **midwifery services** were upgraded by 2015, according to the United Nations Population Fund.

___

10 million hectares of farmland are lost every year due to **ecosystem degradation**.

___

CHAPTER 3
ECONOMIC AND
SOCIAL DEVELOPMENT

DEVELOPMENT:
A PRIORITY FOR THE UNITED NATIONS

Although most people associate the United Nations with issues of peace and security, a huge portion of the Organization's resources are in fact devoted to advancing the Charter's pledge to "promote higher standards of living, full employment, and conditions of economic and social progress and development". The United Nations is guided in its endeavours by the conviction that lasting international peace and security are possible only if the economic and social well-being of people everywhere is assured.

POVERTY AND DEVELOPMENT

Development implies that the quality of life for individuals, families and communities is improving, which in turn allows people to become more productive. Increased productivity places a country in a better position to trade with other countries,

WHAT POVERTY MEANS

Poverty is more than a lack of money. It is a pronounced deprivation of well-being.

Poverty means having insufficient food and basic nutrition, limited or inexistent access to health services and education, a lack of freedom and representation.

Poverty is also a fear of tomorrow, allowing people to only think about living one day at a time.

Poverty means marginalization. Poor people are often treated as invisible, voiceless and powerless to improve their living conditions.

and more trade means more goods and services to continue improving the living conditions of more people.

Development is a complex process, though. Reaching an acceptable standard of living for all includes giving everyone access to the basics: food, housing, jobs, health services, education, safety and security. A country must concurrently pay attention to social, economic, political, cultural and environmental issues to ensure that development is sustainable and beneficial to all.[2]

Development is also a human right, as per the Declaration on the Right to Development of 1986. You will find more information on this in chapter five.

GLOBALIZATION

Globalization is not new: people have been travelling to other parts of the world and trading goods and services for millennia. This process brings the world closer through the exchange of products, information, knowledge and culture. Over the last few decades, though, the integration of economies and societies around the world has happened at a much faster and more dramatic pace because of unprecedented advancements in technology, communications, science, transport and industry.[3]

While globalization is a catalyst for and a consequence of human progress, it is also a difficult process that creates significant challenges and problems and therefore requires adjustments. Many people have criticized the effects of globalization, stressing that inequalities in the current global trading system hurt some countries more than others, some people more than others and some job sectors more than others. They say that the process has exploited people in developing countries while axing jobs in the developed world, caused massive disruptions and produced only a few benefits for too few people at the top of the social pyramid. Supporters of globalization, on the other hand, say that the opening up of countries like China, Vietnam, India and Uganda to the world economy has significantly reduced poverty.

For all countries to be able to reap the benefits of globalization, the international community must continue working to reduce distortions in international trade (for instance, cutting agricultural subsidies and trade barriers) that favour developed countries, in order to create a fairer system for everybody.

---

[2]   See World Bank, "Issues: Development," Youthink! *http://youthink.worldbank.org/issues/development*

[3]   Ibid

A UNDP project helped empower herder groups in Mongolia, improving their livelihood while protecting the biodiversity of the region.

UNITED NATIONS ACTION

Issues such as refugee population flows, organized crime, terrorism, drug trafficking, AIDS and other epidemics and, of course, climate change are not limited to one country in isolation. They are global challenges requiring coordinated international action. The impact of persistent poverty and unemployment in one region can quickly be felt in others, due to migration, social disruption and conflict.

Similarly, in the age of a global economy, financial instability in one country is immediately felt in the markets of others. There is also a growing consensus on the role played by democracy, human rights, popular participation, good governance and the empowerment of women in fostering economic and social development. This awakening has been exemplified and illustrated in a dramatic manner by the revolutions that spread around the Middle East and North Africa in 2011-2012, which many say were fuelled in part by the increased use of social media sites such as Facebook and Twitter.

DID YOU KNOW?

INVESTING IN WOMEN HELPS ERADICATE POVERTY FASTER

Women perform 66 per cent of the world's work and produce 50 per cent of the food, but they earn only 10 per cent of the income and own just 1 per cent of the property.

When girls are able to obtain a secondary education, a country's economy grows through women's increased participation in the labour force and their productivity and earnings. When an educated girl earns an income, she reinvests 90 per cent of it in her family—an extremely high number compared to boys, who devote 35 per cent of their income to their families.

Education and work give women increased influence and power to make decisions in the household. Maternal health and children's education and nutrition are all dependent upon how well limited resources are accessed, allocated and used.

The United Nations provided these women with a diesel engine powering a variety of equipment, so they no longer spend their days gathering firewood. Instead, they now sell the mango and sweet potato jam they produce, allowing them to earn much-needed income.

Obstacles and challenges to development know no borders. With its 193 Member States, the United Nations provides a platform for discussion and formulation of developmental policies. To focus attention on certain issues, the United Nations organizes global conferences and promotes international development days, years and decades. As the global centre for consensus building, the United Nations has set priorities for international cooperation, such as the Millennium Development Goals, to assist countries in their efforts and to foster a supportive environment. United Nations development efforts have profoundly affected the lives and well-being of millions of people throughout the world.

MILLENNIUM DEVELOPMENT GOALS

At the United Nations Millennium Summit held in September 2000 in New York, 189 world leaders endorsed the Millennium Declaration, a commitment to a new global partnership to reduce extreme poverty and build a safer, more prosperous and equitable world.

The Declaration was translated into a road map setting out eight time-bound goals to be reached by 2015, known as the Millennium Development Goals (MDGs). The eight MDGs break down into 20 quantifiable targets that are measured by 60 indicators. They provide concrete, numerical benchmarks for tackling extreme poverty in its many dimensions.

THE EIGHT GOALS

To assess the progress made since 2000, the Secretary-General called for a summit on the MDGs in 2010, which concluded with the adoption of a global action plan to achieve the eight goals by their 2015 target date. World leaders agreed to ensure women and girls equal access to education, basic services, health care, economic opportunities and decision making at all levels, recognizing that the achievement of the MDGs depends largely on women's empowerment. They also stressed that accelerated action on the goals requires sustainable, inclusive and equitable economic growth—growth that enables everyone to benefit from progress and share in economic opportunities.

FOCUS ON

THE MILLENNIUM DEVELOPMENT GOALS TO ACHIEVE BY THE YEAR 2015

Goal 1: Eradicate extreme poverty and hunger

Targets:

» Halve, between 1990 and 2015, the proportion of people whose income is less than $1 a day

» Achieve full and productive employment and decent work for all, including women and young people

» Halve, between 1990 and 2015, the proportion of people who suffer from hunger

Goal 2: Achieve universal primary education

Target:

» Ensure that, by 2015, children everywhere, boys and girls alike, will be able to complete a full course of primary schooling

Goal 3: Promote gender equality and empower women

Target:

» Eliminate gender disparity in primary and secondary education, preferably by 2005, and in all levels of education no later than 2015

Goal 4: Reduce child mortality

Target:

» Reduce by two thirds, between 1990 and 2015, the mortality rate of children under five years of age

Goal 5: Improve maternal health

Targets:

» Reduce by three quarters, between 1990 and 2015, the maternal mortality ratio

» Achieve, by 2015, universal access to reproductive health care

Goal 6: Combat HIV/AIDS, malaria and other diseases

Targets:

» Halt and begin to reverse, by 2015, the spread of HIV/AIDS

» Achieve, by 2010, universal access to treatment for HIV/AIDS for all those who need it

» Halt and begin to reverse, by 2015, the incidence of malaria and other major diseases

Goal 7: Ensure environmental sustainability

Targets:

» Integrate the principles of sustainable development into country policies and programmes and reverse the loss of environmental resources

» Reduce biodiversity loss, achieving, by 2010, a significant reduction in the rate of loss

» Halve, by 2015, the proportion of the population without sustainable access to safe drinking water and basic sanitation

» Achieve, by 2020, a significant improvement in the lives of at least 100 million slum dwellers

Goal 8: Develop a global partnership for development

Targets:

» Develop further an open, rule-based, predictable, non-discriminatory trading and financial system

» Address the special needs of least developed countries, landlocked countries and small island developing States

» Deal comprehensively with developing countries' debt

» In cooperation with pharmaceutical companies, provide access to affordable, essential drugs in developing countries

» In cooperation with the private sector, make available benefits of new technologies, especially Information and Communication Technologies (ICTs)

WHERE DO WE STAND?

The Millennium Declaration and the Goals derived from it have inspired development efforts and helped to set global and national priorities and to focus subsequent actions. While more work lies ahead, the world has cause to celebrate, in part due to the continued economic growth of some developing countries and targeted interventions in critical areas. Increased funding from many sources has translated into the expansion of programmes to deliver services and resources to those most in need.

However, progress has not been achieved equally, and some efforts need to be intensified. Disparities between urban and rural areas remain daunting. We must also continue to target the people who are hardest to reach: the poorest of the poor and those disadvantaged because of their sex, age, ethnicity or disability.

The achievements and setbacks of each goal are detailed below, target by target.

GOAL 1: Eradicate extreme poverty and hunger

Target: Halve, between 1990 and 2015, the proportion of people whose income is less than $1 a day

Despite setbacks caused by the 2008-09 financial crisis and the continuing recession, as well as the effects of the recent food and energy crises, the world is on track to meet the MDG target of halving the proportion of people living on less than $1 a day.

> » Robust growth in the first half of the 2000-2010 decade reduced the number of people in developing countries living on less than $1.25 a day from about 1.8 billion in 1990 to 1.4 billion in 2005. At the same time, poverty dropped from 46 to 27 per cent.

> » By 2015, the number of people in developing countries living on less than $1.25 a day is projected to fall below 900 million.

Target: Achieve full and productive employment and decent work for all, including women and young people

Economic recovery has failed to translate into employment opportunities, so it will be difficult to reach the full-employment target by 2015.

The majority of the working poor live in rural areas and depend on agriculture for subsistence.

Developed regions are not generating sufficient employment opportunities to absorb growth in the working-age population. Between 2007 and 2010, their employment-to-population ratio dropped from 56.8 to 54.8 per cent, while that of developing regions remained mostly unchanged.

» According to the International Labour Organization, one in five workers and their families worldwide were living in extreme poverty in 2009.

Furthermore:

» For a staggering 1.3 billion people who make up over 40 per cent of the global workforce, earnings are too low to lift them and their dependants above the poverty threshold of $2 per day.

» Agriculture is still the single largest employer in the world, with 1.3 billion farmers and agricultural workers in total.

» Agriculture is the largest source of income and jobs for poor rural households, and often their surest path out of poverty. Smallholder farms, most still rain-fed, provide up to 80 per cent of the food in developing countries, so investing in their productivity is an important way to increase food production.

Conflicts, financial and economic crises and rising food prices all contribute to hunger. A hungry person is weak, tired and unable to concentrate, study or work. Hunger leads to illness. The body starts to feed on itself, eventually leading to starvation and death.

Target: *Halve, between 1990 and 2015, the proportion of people who suffer from hunger*

Based on the progress made so far, and in light of the financial crisis and rising food prices, it will be difficult to meet the hunger-reduction target in many regions of the developing world.

» Chronic hunger still affected 925 million people in 2010.

» The proportion of people in the developing world who went hungry in 2005-2007 remained stable at 16 per cent, despite significant reductions in extreme poverty.

» About one in four children under the age of 5 is underweight in the developing world, down from almost one in three in 1990.

THERE IS ENOUGH FOOD FOR EVERYONE GLOBALLY

One in nearly seven people is going hungry. One in three children is underweight. Why are 925 million people in the world going hungry when food has never before existed in such abundance? There are a number of different causes:

» Natural disasters such as floods, tropical storms and severe droughts (the single most common cause of food shortages in the world) are on the rise and have calamitous consequences for food security in poor, developing countries.

» Climate change causes more parts of the world to suffer from natural disasters and exacerbates already adverse natural conditions in others.

» Conflict and war turn food into a weapon. Aggressors starve opponents into submission, seizing or destroying their food and livestock. Markets are wrecked and fields and water wells are often mined or contaminated, forcing farmers to abandon their land.

» Poverty traps people in a cycle of hunger and poverty. Often the poor don't have enough money to buy food or the seeds or tools they need to grow it. They also may not have the land, water or education to lay the foundations for a secure future.

» Agricultural infrastructure, such as roads, warehouses and irrigation, is key to eradicating poverty and hunger. Without this, high transport costs, lack of storage facilities and unreliable water supplies limit agricultural yields and access to food.

» Poor farming practices, deforestation, overcropping and overgrazing are exhausting the Earth's fertility and spreading the roots of hunger. The world's fertile farmland is under threat from erosion, salination and desertification.

WFP planes deliver food to people in crisis on a daily basis.

Goal 2: Achieve universal primary education

Target: Ensure that, by 2015, children everywhere, boys and girls alike, will be able to complete a full course of primary schooling

To achieve universal primary education, children everywhere must complete a full cycle of primary schooling. Current statistics show that the world will not meet this goal by 2015.

Only 87 out of every 100 children in developing regions complete primary receive an education.

» There were still 67 million children out of school in 2009, down from 106 million in 1999. Almost half of these children live in sub-Saharan Africa and a quarter in Southern Asia.

» In half of the least developed countries, at least two out of five children in primary school drop out before reaching the last grade.

Furthermore:

» The literacy rate of youth (ages 15 to 24) worldwide increased from 83 to 89 per cent between 1990 and 2009. In spite of overall progress, 127 million young people lacked basic reading and writing skills in 2009.

» It is estimated that double the current number of teachers would be needed in sub-Saharan Africa to meet the primary education target by 2015.

All children—boys and girls alike—need an education. It is their right and, for most, their way out of extreme poverty.

Goal 3: Promote gender equality and empower women

Target: *Eliminate gender disparity in primary and secondary education, preferably by 2005, and in all levels of education no later than 2015*

Girls are gaining ground when it comes to education, though unequal access persists in many regions. The target is within reach.

In developing regions, 96 girls were enrolled in primary and secondary school for every 100 boys in 2009. This is a significant improvement compared to 1999, when only 88 girls were enrolled.

FOCUS ON

GIRLS' EDUCATION: LEELA GOES TO SCHOOL[4]

When you educate a girl, you educate a family. When you educate a family, you educate a nation. Despite this, millions of girls are denied this basic human right.

In India, where poverty is still widespread, many girls under the age of 14 do not go to school. They are expected to prepare for marriage, help with household chores and work in the fields. Leela is an exception.

Leela is a bubbly 11-year-old with an infectious laugh. She lives with her mother, grandmother and two siblings in one room in a densely populated Mumbai slum, where public facilities are scarce and open sewers abound.

Leela's mother works very hard, sometimes skipping meals, to send Leela to one of the best government-aided private girls schools in Mumbai. "I don't want my children to have a life like mine," says Leela's mother. "I want them to study, be independent, make something of themselves."

Leela loves going to school. She dreams of becoming a teacher. She sometimes gives lessons to other children who do not go to school. At school, uniforms help the girls see past surface differences. Everyone, rich or poor, is equal.

Leela's teacher stresses the value of education for girls, "Once you have an education," she tells her pupils, "you'll stand on your own feet." Leela is determined to make her dream come true. She cites Indira Gandhi, India's first female prime minister and the second female Head of Government in the world, as a role model.

---

4   UN Works—For People and the Planet, "Girls' Education in India," *http://www.un.org/works*

» The gender parity (equality) index for the whole developing world is highest, at 97 girls for every 100 boys, at the tertiary level of education (college or university).

» In Eastern Asia, girls slightly outnumber boys in primary and secondary schools.

Furthermore:

» The share of women in non-agricultural paid employment worldwide increased from 35 per cent in 1990 to almost 40 per cent in 2009.

» In 2010, the world economy began to recover from the 2008-2009 financial crisis, and unemployment started to decrease among both sexes; however, the unemployment rate for men has declined faster than that for women. The gap between women and men in many regions will not close any time soon.

» By the end of January 2011, women held 19.3 per cent of seats in single or lower houses of parliament worldwide. This is an all-time high. Yet despite the growing numbers, the target of equal participation of women and men in politics is still far off. Around the same time, women accounted for only 13.4 per cent of presiding officers in parliament, and just 10 countries had female Heads of State, 13 female Heads of Government.

Goal 4: Reduce child mortality

Target: Reduce by two thirds, between 1990 and 2015, the mortality rate of children under five years of age

Increasing evidence suggests that the target can be reached, but only with substantial and accelerated action to eliminate the leading killers of children, namely malnutrition, improper postnatal care, diarrhoea, malaria and pneumonia.

» Globally, the mortality rate for children under 5 years of age has declined by 35 per cent, from 88 deaths per 1,000 live births in 1990 to 57 in 2010.

The number of deaths of children under 5 years of age worldwide declined from 12 million in 1990 to 7.6 million in 2010, which translates to nearly 12,000 fewer children dying each day.

» Children in rural areas are more at risk of dying, even in regions where child mortality is low.

» Between 2000 and 2008, the combination of improved immunization coverage and the opportunity for a second dose led to a 78 per cent drop in measles deaths worldwide. These averted deaths represent one quarter of the decline in mortality from all causes among children under 5 years of age.

Furthermore:

» New vaccines against the leading causes of child deaths—pneumonia and diarrhoea—offer renewed hope. By themselves, these vaccines could save about one million children's lives every year, sharply increasing the 2.5 million under 5 years of age deaths currently prevented by immunization annually.

» In all developing regions, children of mothers with some degree of education are at less risk of dying. A child's chances of survival increase even further if his or her mother has a secondary or higher education.

Goal 5: Improve maternal health

Target: *Reduce by three quarters, between 1990 and 2015, the maternal mortality ratio*

Despite progress, pregnancy remains a major health risk for women in many developing countries. The MDG target is still far off.

» In the developing regions as a whole, the maternal mortality ratio dropped by 34 per cent between 1990 and 2008, from 440 maternal deaths per 100,000 live births to 290.

» In 2008, there were still 640 maternal deaths per 100,000 live births in sub-Saharan Africa, versus 17 in developed regions.

» Maternal deaths are concentrated in sub-Saharan Africa and Southern Asia, which together accounted for 87 per cent of such deaths globally in 2008.

Target: *Achieve, by 2015, universal access to reproductive health*

Progress in this area slowed from 2000 to 2008 in almost all regions, meaning it's unlikely the MDG target will be met. The number of women of reproductive age in developing regions has risen by nearly 50 per cent since 1990, so family-planning programmes and health-care services need to invest more to simply keep pace with the growing number of women.

In developing regions overall, the proportion of deliveries performed by skilled health personnel rose from 55 per cent in 1990 to 65 per cent in 2009.

» Since 1990, the proportion of women receiving antenatal care has increased substantially worldwide. In developing regions, the share of pregnant women attended to at least once during pregnancy increased from 64 per cent in 1990 to 81 per cent in 2009. The proportion of women receiving the recommended number of visits in developing regions remains low, but progress is being made, with an increase from 35 per cent in 1990 to 51 per cent in 2009.

» Sub-Saharan Africa has the highest birth rate among adolescents (122 births per 1,000 women), which has changed little since 1990.

» By 2008, more than half of women aged 15 to 49 who were married or in a union were using some form of contraception in all but two regions— sub-Saharan Africa and Oceania.

» Worldwide, more than 120 million women aged 15 to 49 who are married or in a union have an unmet need for help with family planning.

Goal 6: Combat HIV/AIDS, malaria and other diseases

Target: Halt and begin to reverse, by 2015, the spread of HIV/AIDS

The spread has already been halted and begun to reverse. This MDG target has been achieved.

» Between 2001 and 2009, the HIV incidence rate declined steadily, by nearly 25 per cent worldwide.

» In 2009, an estimated 2.6 million people were infected with HIV. This represents a drop of 21 per cent since 1997, the year in which new infections peaked.

» Globally, nearly 23 per cent of all people living with HIV are under the age of 25. Young people (aged 15 to 24) account for 41 per cent of new infections among those aged 15 or older.

» In 2009, women represented a slight majority (about 51 per cent) of people living with HIV.

» Understanding how HIV spreads is the first step to avoiding infection. On average, only 33 per cent of young men and 20 per cent of young women in developing regions have a comprehensive and correct knowledge of HIV.

Furthermore:

» According to UNAIDS, nearly 30 million people have died of AIDS-related causes since the first case of AIDS was reported on 5 June 1981.

» Globally, in 2009, about 16.6 million children were estimated to have lost one or both parents to AIDS, up from 14.6 million in 2005; 89 per cent of those children live in sub-Saharan Africa.

FOCUS ON

HIV/AIDS: GETTING TO ZERO— ZERO NEW INFECTIONS, ZERO AIDS-RELATED DEATHS, ZERO DISCRIMINATION

The new UNAIDS strategy intends to reach the following goals by 2015:

Zero new infections

» Reduce by half the sexual transmission of HIV, including among young people and sex workers.

» Eliminate vertical (mother-to-child) transmission of HIV and reduce by half AIDS-related maternal mortalities.

» Prevent all new HIV infections among people who use drugs.

Zero AIDS-related deaths

» Provide universal access to antiretroviral therapy for people living with HIV who are eligible for treatment.

» Reduce by half tubercolosis deaths among people living with HIV.

» Address the needs of people living with and households affected by HIV in all social-protection strategies and ensure access to essential care and support.

Zero discrimination

» Reduce by half the number of countries with punitive laws and practices around HIV transmission, sex work, drug use or gay relationships, all of which block effective responses.

» Eliminate HIV-related restrictions on entry, stay and residence in half of the countries that have such restrictions.

» Ensure that the HIV-specific needs of women and girls are addressed in at least half of all national HIV responses.

» Enforce a zero-tolerance policy for gender-based violence.

Target: *Achieve, by 2010, universal access to treatment for HIV/AIDS for all those who need it*

Treatment for HIV and AIDS has expanded quickly, but not fast enough to meet the 2010 target for universal access.

» In 2009, the World Health Organization (WHO) revised its guidelines for treatment of adults and adolescents with HIV, including pregnant women. As a result, the number of people defined as needing antiretroviral therapy grew, from 10.1 million to 14.6 million at the end of 2009. Based on the new guidelines, coverage of antiretroviral therapy increased from 28 per cent in December 2008 to 36 per cent at the end of 2009. Under the previous 2006 guidelines, global coverage would have reached 52 per cent in 2009.

The number of people receiving antiretroviral treatment for HIV or AIDS increased thirteenfold from 2004 to 2009. As a result, the number of AIDS-related deaths declined by 19 per cent over the same period.

» In 2010, 34 million people were living with the virus—a 31 per cent increase over 1999.

» By the end of 2009, 5.25 million people were receiving antiretroviral therapy for HIV or AIDS in low- and middle-income countries, compared with 0.4 million in 2003.

» About 356,400 children under age 15 were receiving antiretroviral therapy at the end of 2009, up from 275,300 at the end of 2008. These children represented an estimated 28 per cent of all children under 15 who needed treatment in low- and middle-income countries, up from 22 per cent in 2008.

» Without treatment, approximately one third of children born to women living with HIV will become infected in the womb, at birth or through breastfeeding. Some 53 per cent of pregnant women living with HIV received antiretroviral medicines in 2009, up from 45 per cent in 2008.

Target: *Halt and begin to reverse, by 2015, the incidence of malaria and other major diseases*

Major advances are being made against malaria and tuberculosis. If these trends continue, the world is on track to achieve the MDG target.

Globally, deaths from malaria are down by an estimated 20 per cent, from nearly 985,000 in 2000 to 781,000 in 2009. Over the same period of time, the number of

Insecticidal nets can provide malaria protection for at-risk groups.

malaria cases first rose, from about 233 million in 2000 to 244 million in 2005, and then decreased, to 225 million in 2009.

» 90 per cent of all deaths from malaria still occur in sub-Saharan Africa.

» In 2008, malaria killed a child every 45 seconds.

» Between 2008 and 2010, 290 million mosquito nets were distributed in sub-Saharan Africa, enough to cover 76 per cent of the 765 million people at risk in 2010.

» An estimated 9.4 million people worldwide were newly diagnosed with tuberculosis in 2009, the same number as in 2008.

» In 2009, tuberculosis caused an estimated 1.3 million deaths among people who were not infected with HIV. An additional 0.4 million deaths from tuberculosis were recorded among people who were HIV-positive.

» Between 1995 and 2009, a total of 41 million tuberculosis patients were successfully treated according to the World Health Organization's Stop TB Strategy; up to six million lives were saved as a result.

Goal 7: Ensure environmental sustainability

Target: Integrate the principles of sustainable development into country policies and programmes and reverse the loss of environmental resources

Progress has been made towards more sustainable development, but human activities still threaten the environment and its resources. It's likely that the MDG target will only be partially met.

Forests are disappearing rapidly in South America and Africa, while Asia—led by China—registers net gains.

» The net change in forest area over the period 2000-2010 is estimated at an annual loss of 5.2 million hectares, down from a loss of 8.3 million hectares annually between 1990 and 2000.

» According to the World Meteorological Organization, 2001-2010 was the warmest decade on record since 1880 in terms of average global temperatures. It topped the previous record decade, 1991-2000.

 FOCUS ON

FROM BIG WORDS TO SMALL FISH[5]

Jon Bjornsson and Thor Jonsson are fishermen based in Keflavik, Iceland.

"For us, the United Nations Convention on the Law of the Sea has really meant the difference between economic survival and unemployment", they say. "It used to be that vessels would come from all parts of the world to fish around here. With this small ship that Jon and I operate, we could not compete against these huge fishing armadas. But the Convention clearly states now that these waters are for our and other Icelanders' exclusive use."

The United Nations encourages the progressive development of international law and its codification. The Convention on the Law of the Sea has been especially important, entering into force in 1994 after decades of work by the United Nations. Among other things, the Convention stipulates that coastal States have sovereign rights over natural resources and certain economic activities in exclusive 200-nautical-mile economic zones along their shores.

---

5   United Nations Cyberschoolbus, "The United Nations in Our Daily Lives," *http:// cyberschoolbus.un.org*

» Despite the downturn in economic activity, global greenhouse gas emissions continue their ascent. Emissions in 2008 were 38 per cent above the 1990 level.

» The proportion of overexploited, depleted or recovering fish stocks increased from 10 per cent in the mid-1970s to 33 per cent in 2008. Overfishing, pollution and loss of habitat remain the most serious pressures on fisheries.

» Most regions withdraw less than 25 per cent of their renewable water resources, but the limits for sustainable water resources have already been exceeded in Western Asia and Northern Africa.

Target: *Reduce biodiversity loss, achieving, by 2010, a significant reduction in the rate of loss*

The world missed the 2010 target. Despite increased investment in the issue, the main causes of biodiversity loss—high rates of consumption, habitat loss, the spread of invasive species, pollution and climate change—are not being sufficiently addressed. Biodiversity is vitally important; billions of people rely directly on diverse species for their livelihoods and often their survival.

The unrestricted exploitation of wildlife has led to the disappearance of many animal species at an alarming rate, destroying earth's biological diversity and upsetting the ecological balance.

The rich biodiversity of the world's forests remains imperilled by the continually high rate of global deforestation and forest degradation, as well as a decline in primary forests. One positive trend, however, is growth in the establishment of protected areas, which increased by 94 million hectares since 1990 and now cover an estimated 13 per cent of the world's forests.

> » In 2010, over 150,000 protected sites covered 12.7 per cent of the world's land area and 7.2 per cent of its coastal waters (extending out to 12 nautical miles). Beyond this, marine protection remains very limited.

> » The global tide of extinctions continues unabated. Amphibians such as rare species of frogs are most threatened and are declining at an alarming rate, but birds and mammals with known trends show deterioration as well.

> » Nearly 17,000 species of plants and animals are currently at risk of extinction, and the number of species threatened by extinction is growing every day.

Target: Halve, by 2015, the proportion of the population without sustainable access to safe drinking water and basic sanitation

The world is likely to surpass the drinking water target—though more than 1 in 10 people may still be without access in 2015—but it is far from meeting the sanitation target. In fact, at the current rate of progress, it will take until 2049 to provide 77 per cent of the global population with flush toilets and other forms of improved sanitation.

Unsafe water brings death or diseases like cholera, malaria and diarrhoea. Yet more than one in every seven people does not yet have safe drinking water.

» Globally, access to clean drinking water increased from 77 per cent in 1990 to 87 per cent in 2008.

» Still, 884 million people worldwide do not have access to safe drinking water. In 2008, an estimated 141 million urbanites and 743 million rural dwellers continued to rely on unimproved sources for their daily drinking water needs.

» Almost half the population of developing regions and some 2.6 billion people globally were not using an improved form of sanitation in 2008.

» In 2008, an estimated 1.1 billion people did not use any facility at all and practised open defecation. This poses enormous health risks, particularly for poorer segments of the population, who are most exposed to the dangers of inadequate human waste disposal.

» Globally, an urban resident is 1.7 times more likely to use an improved sanitation facility than someone living in a rural area.

Target: *Achieve, by 2020, a significant improvement in the lives of at least 100 million slum dwellers*

The target has already been achieved twice over. From 2000 to 2010, more than 200 million slum dwellers gained access to either improved water, sanitation and/or durable and less crowded housing.

From 2000 to 2010, the share of urban residents in the developing world living in slums declined from 39 per cent to 33 per cent.

» In absolute terms, the number of slum dwellers continues to grow, due in part to the fast pace of urbanization. The number of urban residents living in slum conditions is now estimated at some 828 million, compared to 657 million in 1990 and 767 million in 2000.

Furthermore:

» The world is inexorably becoming urban. By 2030, all developing regions, including Asia and Africa, will have more people living in urban than rural areas.

» Improved conditions in housing, water and sanitation will not only save lives among the very poor, but also support progress in education and health.

» UN-HABITAT estimates confirm that the progress made on the slum target has not been enough to counter the demographic expansion of informal settlements in the developing world.

According to UN-Habitat, the urban population grows by two people every second. One out of three urban dwellers—so, over one billion people—are living in slum conditions.

Goal 8: Develop a global partnership for development

United Nations Member States, together with international institutions and non-State actors in civil society and the private sector, have forged a global partnership for development. This partnership has produced important achievements, including a record volume of Official Development Assistance (ODA) in 2010, increased aid to the Least Developed Countries (LDCs) and other forms of cooperation for the development of poorer countries. Still, there is reason for concern about the rate and scale of progress as 2015 draws closer.

Target: Develop further an open, rule-based, predictable, non-discriminatory trading and financial system

Despite the past few years of troubling economic times, protectionism has been averted due to strong international cooperation. Protectionism results from government actions and policies that restrict or restrain international trade, often with the intent of protecting national businesses from foreign competition.

» About 80 per cent of exports from developing countries are now imported free from customs duties in developed countries.

» All but one of the developed countries have granted duty-free market access to at least 97 per cent of products originating from the poorest countries. The exception is the United States, which maintains tariffs on imports of textiles and clothing from Asian least developed countries.

Target: *Address the special needs of least developed countries, landlocked countries and small island developing States*

Aid to developing countries is at a record high but still falls short of promises made in 2005.

» Donor countries provided a record $129 billion in ODA in 2010; however, much of it has yet to be delivered.

» In 2010, Denmark, Luxembourg, the Netherlands, Norway and Sweden continued to exceed the United Nations target for ODA of 0.7 per cent of their gross national incomes.

» The United States, France, the United Kingdom, Germany and Japan were the largest donors by volume.

» Between 2009 and 2010, Australia, Belgium, Canada, Japan, Portugal, the Republic of Korea and the United Kingdom made the largest increases in actual amounts of ODA.

» Due to fiscal constraints in several donor countries, the growth of ODA is expected to slow to about 2 per cent per year during 2011-2013, compared to 8 per cent annually over the previous three years.

» Aid increasingly goes to the poorest countries, with the LDCs receiving about a third of donors' total assistance today.

Target: *Deal comprehensively with developing countries' debt*

A sharp drop in exports in 2009 interrupted the trend of developing countries' being able to service debt in time.

» A country's external debt burden affects its creditworthiness and vulnerability to economic shocks. Better debt management, the expansion of trade and, particularly for the poorest countries, substantial debt relief have reduced their burden.

» Between 2000 and 2008, the average ratio of public debt service to exports for developing regions declined from 12.5 to 3.4 per cent, but rose again to 3.6 per cent in 2009, due to the global economic crisis and a resultant drop in export earnings.

» As of mid-May 2011, the International Monetary Fund (IMF) identified 19 countries that were in debt distress or at high risk of debt distress.

Target: In cooperation with pharmaceutical companies, provide access to affordable, essential drugs in developing countries

Making essential medicines more affordable and accessible will require stronger and more complex measures at the local, national, regional and international levels, as well as greater collaboration between the public and private sectors.

Essential medicines are available in only 42 per cent of facilities in the public sector, compared to 64 per cent in the private sector.

» Many countries lack the national regulatory capacity to ensure the quality of medicines, and thus populations remain vulnerable to less effective treatments.

» The availability of medicines to treat non-communicable diseases is even lower than that for communicable diseases.

» Since the majority of medicine purchases in low- and middle-income countries are made out of pocket, affordability is a key determinant of access. Substantial shares of the populations in many low- and middle-income countries can be impoverished by the costs of purchasing medicine.

Target: In cooperation with the private sector, make available benefits of new technologies, especially Information and Communication Technologies (ICTs)

The world is increasingly interconnected through mobile, high-speed communications.

» By the end of 2010, 90 per cent of the world's inhabitants were covered by a mobile cellular signal.

» At the same time, the number of mobile cellular subscriptions had grown to an estimated 5.3 billion—including nearly one billion subscriptions to 3G (third generation) services—and more than two billion people worldwide were using the Internet, increasingly through broadband access.

Many developed countries are reaching saturation levels in mobile cellular subscriptions, with an average penetration level (active mobile phone numbers) of 116 per cent. Growth in mobile telephony continues to be strong in the developing world, where mobile penetration had reached around 68 per cent by the end of 2010.

» In 2012, one out of three people worldwide connected to the Internet regularly.

» In absolute numbers, developed regions have been surpassed by the developing world, which in 2010 accounted for 60 per cent of Internet users worldwide, up from 40 per cent in 2005.

» By the end of 2010, fixed broadband penetration in developed regions averaged 24.6 per cent, compared to only 4.4 per cent in the developing world.

» Mobile broadband has started to become a true alternative to fixed broadband access, which is often unavailable or prohibitively expensive. In 2010, 143 countries were offering mobile broadband services commercially, compared to less than 50 in 2005.

The world is rapidly interconnected through high-speed communications.

MILLENNIUM DEVELOPMENT GOALS: 2012 PROGRESS CHART

The progress chart operates on two levels. The words in each box indicate the present degree of compliance with the target. The colours show progress towards the target according to the legend below:

Green: *Target already met or expected to be met by 2015.*

Yellow: *Progress insufficient to reach the target if prevailing trends persist.*

Red: *No progress or deterioration.*

Beige: *Missing or insufficient data.*

Goals and Targets	Africa		Asia				Oceania	Latin America & Carib-bean	Caucasus & Central Asia
	Northern	Sub-Saharan	Eastern	South-Eastern	Southern	Western			
GOAL 1 — Eradicate extreme poverty and hunger									
Reduce extreme poverty by half	low poverty	very high poverty	moderate poverty	high poverty	very high poverty	low poverty	very high poverty	moderate poverty	low poverty
Productive and decent employment	large deficit in decent work	very large deficit in decent work	large deficit in decent work	large deficit in decent work	very large deficit in decent work	large deficit in decent work	very large deficit in decent work	moderate deficit in decent work	moderate deficit in decent work
Reduce hunger by half	low hunger	very high hunger	moderate hunger	moderate hunger	high hunger	moderate hunger	moderate hunger	moderate hunger	moderate hunger
GOAL 2 — Achieve universal primary education									
Universal primary schooling	high enrol-ment	moderate enrolment	high enrol-ment	high enrol-ment	high enrol-ment	high enrol-ment	–	high enrol-ment	high enrol-ment
GOAL 3 — Promote gender equality and empower women									
Equal girls' enrolment in primary school	close to parity	close to parity	parity	parity	parity	close to parity	close to parity	parity	parity
Women's share of paid employment	low share	medium share	high share	medium share	low share	low share	medium share	high share	high share
Women's equal representation in national parliaments	low represen-tation	moderate representa-tion	moderate represen-tation	low represen-tation	low represen-tation	low represen-tation	very low represen-tation	moderate represen-tation	low represen-tation
GOAL 4 — Reduce child mortality									
Reduce mortality of under-five-year-olds by two thirds	low mortality	high mortality	low mortality	low mortality	moderate mortality	low mortality	moderate mortality	low mortality	moderate mortality

| Goals and Targets | Africa | | Asia | | | | Oceania | Latin America & Carib-bean | Caucasus & Central Asia |
	Northern	Sub-Saharan	Eastern	South-Eastern	Southern	Western			
GOAL 5 — Improve maternal health									
Reduce maternal mortality by three quarters	low mortality	very high mortality	low mortality	moderate mortality	high mortality	low mortality	high mortality	low mortality	low mortality
Access to reproductive health	moderate access	low access	high access	moderate access	moderate access	moderate access	low access	high access	moderate access
GOAL 6 — Combat HIV/AIDS, malaria and other diseases									
Halt and begin to reverse the spread of HIV/ AIDS	low incidence	high incidence	low incidence	low incidence	low incidence	low incidence	low incidence	low incidence	low incidence
Halt and reverse the spread of tuberculosis	low mortality	high mortality	low mortality	moderate mortality	moderate mortality	low mortality	high mortality	low mortality	moderate mortality
GOAL 7 — Ensure environmental sustainability									
Halve proportion of population without improved drinking water	high coverage	low coverage	high coverage	moderate coverage	high coverage	moderate coverage	low coverage	high coverage	moderate coverage
Halve proportion of population without sanitation	high coverage	very low coverage	low coverage	low coverage	very low coverage	moderate coverage	low coverage	moderate coverage	high coverage
Improve the lives of slum-dwellers	moderate propor-tion	very high proportion	moderate propor-tion	high pro-portion	high pro-portion	moderate propor-tion	moderate propor-tion	moderate propor-tion	–
GOAL 8 — Develop a global partnership for development									
Internet users	high usage	moderate usage	high usage	moderate usage	low usage	high usage	low usage	high usage	high usage

For the regional groupings and country data, see mdgs.un.org. Country experiences in each region may differ significantly from the regional average. Due to new data and revised methodologies, this Progress Chart is not comparable with previous versions.

Sources: United Nations, based on data and estimates provided by: Food and Agriculture Organization of the United Nations; Inter-Parliamentary Union; International Labour Organization; International Telecommunication Union; UNAIDS; UNESCO; UN-Habitat; UNICEF; UN Population Division; World Bank; World Health Organization—based on statistics available as of June 2012.

Compiled by Statistics Division, Department of Economic and Social Affairs, United Nations.

DEVELOPMENT FOR TODAY AND TOMORROW

SUSTAINABLE DEVELOPMENT

What is sustainable development?

The world's population of seven billion is likely to increase to nine billion by 2050. The demand for diminishing natural resources is growing. Income gaps are widening. Sustainable development calls for a decent standard of living for everyone today without compromising the needs of future generations. In other words, we must use our resources wisely.

Sustainable development requires us to conserve more and waste less. In industrialized nations, many people live beyond nature's means. For example, one person in a very rich country uses as much energy as 80 people in a very poor country. Overconsumption leads to waste, which pollutes our environment and uses up our resources.

Crushing poverty and growing populations also put great pressure on the environment. When land and forests, which provide food, natural resources and employment,

Human life has a huge impact on the environment as visible and invisible waste pollutes the globe, affecting ecosystems and bringing diseases to—or even causing the deaths of—humans, animals and plants.

are exhausted, people find it harder—sometimes impossible—to survive. Many go to cities, crowding into unhealthy and unsafe slums.

If poor people are forced to destroy their local environments to survive, many generations of people in all countries will suffer the consequences.

Does sustainable development work?

Over the last two decades, there have been many examples of successful sustainable development in the fields of energy, agriculture, urban planning, and production and consumption:

> » In Kenya, innovative finance mechanisms have stimulated new investments in renewable energy sources, including solar, wind, small hydro, biogas and municipal waste energy, generating income and employment.

> » In China, steps to shift to a low-carbon growth strategy based on the development of renewable energy sources have created jobs, income and revenue streams for promising low-carbon industries.

> » In Uganda, a transition to organic agriculture has generated revenue and income for smallholder farmers and benefited the economy, society and environment.

> » In Brazil, a project under the Clean Development Mechanism was adopted in São Paulo to transform two of the city's biggest waste dumps into sustainable landfills. From 2004 to September 2011, the landfills prevented the release into the atmosphere of 352,000 tons of methane, which instead have been used to produce over one million megawatts of electricity.

> » In Nepal, community forestry, led by local groups, contributed to restoring forest resources after a steady decline in the 1990s.

> » In Canada, EcoLogo—one of North America's most respected environmental certification marks—has promoted thousands of products that meet rigorous environmental standards.

> » In France, an estimated 90,000 jobs were created in green sectors between 2006 and 2008, mostly in the fields of energy conservation and the development of renewable energy.

> » In Haiti, the Côte Sud Initiative is expected to benefit an estimated 205,000 people through the recovery and sustainable development of a severely degraded land area about half the size of Greater London.

RIO+20: DEFINING THE FUTURE WE WANT[6]

Rio+20 is the short name for the United Nations Conference on Sustainable Development, that was organized in June 2012 in Rio de Janeiro, Brazil. The objective: to create a safer, more equitable, cleaner, greener and more prosperous world for all.

Twenty years after the 1992 Earth Summit in Rio, where countries adopted Agenda 21—a blueprint to rethink economic growth, advance social equality and ensure environmental protection, the United Nations brought together governments, international institutions and major groups to agree on a range of measures. The goal: to reduce poverty while promoting decent jobs, clean energy and a more sustainable and fair use of resources. Rio+20 provided the chance to move away from business as usual and build a bridge to the future.

Why did we need Rio+20?

> » The world now has seven billion people, and by 2050, there will be nine billion.

> » One out of every five people—1.4 billion total—currently lives on $1.25 a day or less.

> » 1.5 billion people in the world do not have access to electricity.

> » 2.5 billion do not have a toilet.

> » Almost one billion go hungry every day.

> » Greenhouse gas emissions continue to rise, and more than a third of all known species could go extinct if climate change continues unchecked.

If we are to leave a liveable world to our children and grandchildren, the challenges of widespread poverty and environmental destruction need to be tackled now. We will incur far greater costs in the future—including more poverty and instability and a degraded planet—if we fail to adequately address these critical challenges.

Rio+20 provided a successful opportunity to think globally, so that we can all act locally to secure our common future. The Conference considered many sustainable development problems, including challenges related to cities, energy, water, food and ecosystems, and came up with solutions as well as a commitment by 193 States to make those solutions a reality.

---

6   Rio+20: The Future We Want, *http://www.un.org/en/sustainablefuture/*

LINKING ENVIRONMENT AND DEVELOPMENT

The environment is everything that surrounds us. It is the air we breathe, the water we drink, the soil in which we grow our food and all living beings. Development is what we do with these resources to improve our lives.

We change the world—literally

All over the world we do things that we think will make our lives better, but we forget that everything we do changes us and our environment. Sometimes we don't see how connected we are to the Earth and to each other, but the connections are there:

> » Medicines that save lives in Germany may depend on plants that grow in the forests of Costa Rica.

> » Pollution from automobiles in London or Mexico City may affect the climate in Rabat or Tokyo.

> » Carbon dioxide and other gases from factories and cars cause the atmosphere to heat up. This rise in temperature is changing the world's climate.

> » Forests help free the air of carbon dioxide, but many forests are being cut down for their wood or to clear land for farms.

The natural world around us is a fragile place that requires care, respect and knowledge. Air pollution, waterborne diseases, toxic chemicals and natural disasters are just some of the environmental challenges that humankind faces.

Protecting the environment

The United Nations plays a key role in shaping international action to protect our environment, with the United Nations Environment Programme (UNEP) leading these global efforts. The United Nations conducts research, monitors the state of the environment and advises governments on ways to preserve their natural resources. Most importantly, it brings governments together to make international laws to solve particular environmental problems.

Here are some important results of action by the United Nations:

> » The Kyoto Protocol to the Convention on Climate Change (1997) aims to slow global warming. It became a legally binding treaty in 2004. It requires countries to cut harmful greenhouse gasses by 5.2 per cent by 2012.

» The Declaration and Programme of Action for the Sustainable Development of Small Island Developing States (1994) calls on countries to take special action to promote the social and economic development of 40 small island developing States. Many of these small islands have very limited resources and have been unable to reap the benefits of globalization.

» The Convention to Combat Desertification (1994) seeks to resolve problems of overcultivation, deforestation, overgrazing and poor irrigation. One quarter of the Earth's land is threatened by desertification. The livelihoods of over one billion people in more than 100 countries are jeopardized, as farming and grazing land become less productive.

» The United Nations Convention on Biological Diversity (1992) seeks to protect and conserve the wide variety of animal and plant life that is vital for human survival.

Water for life

Water is absolutely essential for life. No living being on the planet can survive without it. It is a prerequisite for human health and well-being as well as for the preservation of the environment.

Women and girls are overwhelmingly the water haulers of the world. This task consumes valuable time and energy, which they could otherwise devote to different types of productive work, childcare and education.

Safe water?

» Globally, 884 million people still do not have access to safe drinking water, and projections show that more than one in 10 people may still be without access in 2015.

» Every year millions of people, most of them children, die from diseases associated with inadequate water supply, sanitation and hygiene.

» Water scarcity, poor water quality and inadequate sanitation negatively impact food security, livelihood choices and educational opportunities for poor families across the world.

» Water-related natural disasters such as floods, tropical storms and tsunamis exact a heavy toll in human life and suffering.

All too regularly, drought afflicts some of the world's poorest countries, exacerbating hunger and malnutrition.

Water and development

Beyond meeting basic human needs, water is a valuable resource. Water supply and sanitation services are critical to sustainable development:

» Water is a major source of energy in some parts of the world, while in others its potential to provide energy remains largely untapped.

» Water is necessary for agriculture and many industrial processes.

» In more than a few countries, it makes up an integral part of transport systems.

» With improved scientific understanding, the international community has come to appreciate more fully the valuable services provided by water-related systems, from flood control to storm protection and water purification.

Water challenges will increase significantly in the coming years. Continuing population growth and rising incomes will lead to greater water consumption, as well as more waste. The urban populations in developing countries will grow dramatically, generating demand well beyond the capacity of already inadequate water supply and sanitation infrastructures and services. According to the United Nations World Water Development Report, by 2050, at least one in four people will likely live in a country affected by chronic or recurring shortages of fresh water.

The importance of biodiversity

Biodiversity and poverty

Biological diversity is at the core of the world's efforts to alleviate poverty. For millennia, humankind has used the Earth's ecosystem to maintain its well-being and fuel economic development. In addition, many belief systems, worldviews and identities centre around biodiversity. Yet despite its fundamental importance, biodiversity continues to be lost at an alarming rate.

Healthy ecosystems provide a variety of goods and services, among them food, medicine, soil formation, air quality, water supply and the cultural and aesthetic value of certain plants and animal species. Protection and proper management of biologically diverse resources is essential to all aspects of sustainable development, especially to the agriculture, livestock, forestry, fishing and tourism sectors.

Biodiversity and development

Today, more than 1.3 billion people depend on biodiversity and basic ecosystem goods and services for their livelihoods. Development does not stop at poverty reduction; environmental sustainability is essential for the achievement of the Millennium Development Goals and the elimination of poverty.

Biodiversity and development are closely linked: biodiversity sustains development, and development impacts biodiversity, either positively or negatively. Although biodiversity does not contribute directly to all sectors of development, sustainable growth cannot be achieved if biodiversity is compromised by development efforts.

Since the poor are particularly dependent on the goods and services supplied by the planet, development strategies that fail to prioritize biodiversity undermine poverty alleviation and are therefore counterproductive.

To highlight the importance of this, the United Nations has adopted a new Strategic Plan for Biodiversity aimed at inspiring broad-based action in support of biodiversity over the next decade. The General Assembly has also declared 2011-2020 the United Nations Decade for Biodiversity.

TEST YOUR KNOWLEDGE

1. What is poverty?

2. How many people are considered to live in extreme poverty?

3. Is globalization a good or bad process? Why?

4. Why does empowering women benefit the whole family and community?

5. What are the Millennium Development Goals?

6. What economic sector is the largest employer worldwide?

7. Name three causes of hunger.

8. What are the leading causes of death for children under the age of five?

9. Which region of the world lags behind most in terms of maternal care?

10. Who is most at risk of becoming infected with HIV?

11. What does the slogan "Getting to Zero" mean?

12. Is malaria a dangerous disease? Why? How can it be avoided?

13. What proportion of the world's population still has no access to safe drinking water? Why is that a problem?

14. Do more people today live in rural or urban areas, and why?

15. What proportion of the world's population is covered by a mobile cellular signal?

16. Why is it so important to protect endangered species of animals and plants?

17. Can you define sustainable development? How does it work?

18. Why should we concern ourselves with protecting the environment?

19. Why is water so vital to life?

20. What is the link between biodiversity and the eradication of poverty?

INTERNATIONAL
PEACE AND SECURITY

QUICK FACTS
ON INTERNATIONAL PEACE AND SECURITY

Since 1948, United Nations-led peacekeeping operations have cost the world a total of about $69 billion; that's 4.23 per cent of **global military spending** for the year 2010 alone, estimated at $1.63 trillion.

_____

Approximately 120,000 soldiers, police officers, volunteers and civilian personnel serve in United Nations **peace operations** in different places around the world today, providing essential security and support to millions of people on four continents.

_____

The United Nations has helped broker over 170 **peace settlements** since its creation.

_____

United Nations **peacebuilding** in post-conflict areas often includes overseeing the collection and destruction of hundreds of thousands of weapons and facilitating the reintegration of former combatants into civil society.

_____

The United Nations played a crucial role in encouraging countries to support the 1997 Ottawa Convention, which advocates a total ban on the production, export and use of **landmines**. The Organization continues to promote universal adherence to this treaty today.

_____

United Nations support has resulted in a wide range of peace and security agreements, including the Nuclear Non-Proliferation Treaty, the Comprehensive Nuclear-Test-Ban Treaty and treaties to establish **nuclear-free zones**.

_____

Of the 34 countries in the world least likely to individually reach the **Millennium Development Goals**, 22 are affected by current or recent conflicts.

_____

Arms kill more than 2,000 men, women and children around the world each day. Eight million light **weapons** and 12 billion bullets are produced each year.

_____

CHAPTER 4

INTERNATIONAL PEACE AND SECURITY

POVERTY CAUSES CONFLICT, WHICH RESULTS IN POVERTY. HOW DO WE BREAK THE CYCLE?

Conflict—whether neighbourhood crime and violence, civil war, or war between two or more countries—is often both a cause and consequence of poverty. Research shows that the combination of poverty, economic decline and dependence on exporting natural resources drives conflict across all regions. Escaping this "conflict trap" remains an elusive goal for many recovering countries: an estimated 40 per cent of which relapse into violence within 10 years.[7]

LOCAL CONSEQUENCES OF A CONFLICT

Conflict is expensive and affects everyone. Within a country, the cost of war continues long after the fighting ends:

» **Deaths** — Combatants make up only a small fraction of overall deaths, injuries and misery. Declining or inexistent health services can lead to more people dying, including non-combatants. About half the deaths resulting from a conflict happen after peace is declared.

» **Flight and disease** — Numerous people flee combat. Refugees often pick up diseases as they escape and spread them across borders as they seek sanctuary.

» **Lost childhoods** — Generations of kids and young people miss out on a stable home, childhood and school. Often they are recruited as soldiers. Once the war ends, it is challenging for these young people to readapt to normal life and think of leading their countries into the future.

---

[7]   See World Bank, Youthink! *http://youthink.worldbank.org/*

» **Landmines** — Mines left in battlefields put land out of use for years, making it difficult for farmers to produce food. Many countries find it too expensive to locate and remove landmines.

» **Poverty and isolation** — Countries that experience civil war often get locked into high levels of military spending and infectious disease, brain and money drain, low growth and entrenched poverty.

THE COST OF CONFLICT IS FELT THROUGHOUT A REGION

Conflicts can also be felt outside the countries directly involved. Neighbouring States and even the rest of the world suffer immediate and long-term consequences:

» **Refugees** — Providing assistance to refugees can strain the economies and health-care systems of neighbouring countries, which often are poor themselves.

» **Infectious diseases** — Refugees often spread diseases like malaria, HIV and tuberculosis.

Conflict destroys homes, tools and fields, exposing survivors to a myriad of threats and depriving them of their means of survival.

» **Economic costs** — Neighbouring countries see their investments dry up and their economic growth decline, make it possible for an existing civil war to spark others or evolve into a regional conflict.

» **Drugs** — About 95 per cent of drug production occurs in civil-war countries, because it is easier to produce large quantities of drugs in places outside the control of a recognized government.

» **HIV/AIDS** — Combatants use mass rape as a weapon to scare and harm civilians, who in turn can contract HIV or other diseases and unknowingly spread infections fast.

» **International terrorism** — Territories without recognized and functional governments become havens for terrorist groups to set up headquarters and training grounds.

THE UNITED NATIONS: CREATED TO KEEP PEACE

The United Nations serves as a global forum where countries can raise and discuss the most difficult issues, including problems of war and peace. When government leaders talk to each other face-to-face, they establish a dialogue, which can result in agreement on how to settle a dispute peacefully. When many countries speak with one voice, by consensus, it creates a global pressure on all. The Secretary-General may also advance a dialogue between and among nations, either directly or through a representative.

PREVENTING CONFLICT

The United Nations has helped prevent many conflicts from flaring up into full-scale wars. It has also negotiated the peaceful settlement of conflicts and on many occasions helped defuse hostilities, for example during the Berlin crisis (1948-1949), the Cuban missile crisis (1962) and the 1973 Middle East crisis. In each of these cases, United Nations intervention helped prevent war between super powers.

The United Nations also played a major role in ending wars in the Congo (1964), between Iran and Iraq (1988), and in El Salvador (1992) and Guatemala (1996). United Nations-led peace settlements have brought sustained economic growth in Mozambique (1994) and independence to Timor-Leste (2002), and in December 2005, the Organization successfully completed its peacekeeping mandate in Sierra Leone.

Patrolling and observing are two of the United Nations peacekeepers' responsibilities on the ground.

OTHER ACCOMPLISHMENTS

The United Nations Transition Assistance Group (UNTAG) supervised Namibia's first free and fair elections, which led to its independence between 1989-1990.

The United Nations Transitional Authority in Cambodia (UNTAC) monitored the ceasefire and the withdrawal of foreign forces from that country, worked with the Cambodian State to set up democratic institutions and organized a free and fair election between 1992-1993.

In the former Yugoslavia, the United Nations Protection Force (UNPROFOR) worked to safeguard civilians in demilitarized zones and enable the delivery of humanitarian assistance during the conflict in the 1990s. Initially established in Croatia, the UNPROFOR mandate was later extended to Bosnia and Herzegovina to support delivery of humanitarian relief and then to the Former Yugoslav Republic of Macedonia for preventive monitoring of borders.

WHAT HAPPENS WHEN A COUNTRY IGNORES THE DECISIONS OF THE SECURITY COUNCIL?

When a country does not comply with the decisions of the Security Council, the Council may take several actions to ensure their implementation. If a country threatens or breaches the peace or commits an act of aggression, the Council may impose economic and trade sanctions, arms and travel bans or diplomatic restrictions. It can also authorize the use of force in certain instances, but that is typically a last resort, to be used only if all peaceful means of settling a dispute have been exhausted.

The Security Council can authorize a coalition of Member States to use "all necessary means," including military action, to deal with a conflict. Examples of this include:

» in 1991, to restore the sovereignty of Kuwait after its invasion by Iraq

» in 1992, to secure the environment for humanitarian relief to be delivered in Somalia

» in 1994, to restore the democratically elected government in Haiti

» in 1999, to restore peace and security in East Timor (Timor-Leste)

 FOCUS ON

THE SECURITY COUNCIL AND THE 2011 CIVIL WAR IN LIBYA

On 17 March 2011, the Security Council approved a "no-fly zone" over Libya, authorizing "all necessary measures" to protect civilians from being attacked by forces loyal to the Gaddafi regime, which was eventually deposed in October of the same year. A number of United Nations Member States joined in the military efforts needed to implement the Council's resolution.

In September 2011, just as the civil war was about to end, the Council agreed to deploy a mission to Libya to support the country's transitional authorities in their reconstruction efforts, which include restoring human rights and the rule of law, drafting a new constitution, promoting reconciliation and preparing for democratic elections. The United Nations Support Mission in Libya (UNSMIL) is not a military mission but a political one, led by the United Nations Department of Political Affairs.

PEACEKEEPING AND PEACEBUILDING

Peacekeeping has traditionally been defined as the use of multinational military forces, under United Nations command, to help control and resolve conflicts between countries. Peacekeeping operations fulfil the role of a neutral third party: they help create and maintain ceasefires and form a buffer zone between warring groups. They also provide a wide range of services, such as electoral assistance, training for local police forces, humanitarian action and help in clearing deadly landmines.

While peacekeepers maintain order on the ground, mediators from the United Nations meet with leaders from the disputing parties and try to reach a peaceful solution.

There are two types of peacekeeping operations: observer missions and peacekeeping forces. Observers are not armed, while soldiers of United Nations peacekeeping forces carry light weapons, which they may use only in self-defence.

Peacekeepers are easily identifiable by the United Nations insignia and the blue berets they wear when on duty. The blue helmet, which has become the symbol of United Nations peacekeepers, is carried during all operations and worn when there is danger. Peacekeepers wear their own national uniforms. Governments that volunteer personnel retain ultimate control over their own military forces serving under the United Nations flag.

MORE INFO

PEACEBUILDING

Peacebuilding usually succeeds peacekeeping and refers to efforts to assist countries and regions in their transitions from war to peace, including activities and programmes to support and strengthen these transitions. A peacebuilding process normally begins with the signing of a peace agreement by former warring parties and a United Nations role in facilitating its success. The UN, through its presence in a country in transition, ensures that difficulties are overcome through negotiation rather than a resort to arms. At the heart of peacebuilding is the attempt to build a new and legitimate State that will have the capacity to peacefully manage disputes, protect its civilians and ensure respect for human rights. Peacebuilding has played a major role in UN operations in Bosnia and Herzegovina, Cambodia, Kosovo, Burundi, Timor-Leste, El Salvador, Sierra Leone and Guatemala, just to cite a few examples.

COMMANDING THE PEACEKEEPING OPERATIONS

Peacekeeping operations are established by the Security Council and directed by the Secretary-General, often through a special representative. When a conflict is first brought before the Council, it usually asks the parties to reach an agreement by peaceful means. If fighting breaks out or persists, the Council tries to secure a ceasefire. Once the ceasefire is secured it may then send a peacekeeping mission to the troubled area.

Does the United Nations have an army?

No, the United Nations has no standing international police or military force. Troops who serve in the United Nations peacekeeping operations are voluntarily contributed by the Member States. Civilians, often drawn from among the United Nations staff, also play a key role in forming such operations.

Zambian peacekeepers from the United Nations Mission in Sudan (UNMIS) walk in front of an armoured patrol in the volatile region of Abyei.

THERE WHEN THE WORLD NEEDS THEM

United Nations peacekeepers make a difference where it matters most. Peacekeeping operations are initiated in response to serious military or humanitarian crises.

The environments into which recent peacekeeping operations have been deployed are among the most difficult and least predictable in the world. These are often extremely hostile and volatile areas where violence is likely to flare up at any given moment, for any reason. United Nations peacekeeping missions deploy where others cannot or are not willing to go and so play a vital role in providing a bridge to stability and eventual peace and development.

In the past, peacekeepers were mainly involved in keeping peace between warring nations. Today, conflict has increasingly become an internal affair as many nations are at war with themselves. Due to civil strife and ethnic conflicts, some governments are unable to exercise authority over large portions of their own territory, causing great human suffering. In such situations, the United Nations is often asked to do two jobs: on the one hand, negotiate a settlement, and on the other, provide emergency relief to the people affected by the conflict. Working under difficult conditions, the United Nations integrates humanitarian assistance with efforts to resolve the crisis so that people can once again live their lives free from fear.

Blue helmets are part of the peacekeepers' equipment and also the nickname for peacekeeping personnel.

UN PEACEKEEPING IN NUMBERS

» 64 years of peacekeeping (1948–2012)

» 66 peacekeeping operations

» 15 current peacekeeping operations, plus one special political mission (as of 31 January 2012)

» over 120,000 people, including close to 99,000 uniformed personnel from 115 countries (as of 31 January 2012), over 17,700 civilian personnel, about 2,300 United Nations Volunteers and 2,200 staff members in the special political mission

» 2,977 fatalities (as of 31 January 2012)

» one Nobel Peace Prize (1988)

» $7.84 billion: total approved budget for 1 July 2011–30 June 2012

» $69 billion: estimated total cost of all operations from 1948 to June 2010

A COST-EFFECTIVE SOLUTION

United Nations peace operations are far less expensive than other forms of international intervention, and their costs are shared more equitably among Member States. The approved peacekeeping budget for the period from 1 July 2011 to 30 June 2012 was approximately $7.84 billion. This represents less than 0.5 per cent of global military spending (estimated at $1.63 trillion in 2010).

When United Nations costs per peacekeeper are compared to the costs of troops deployed by the United States, other developed States, or regional organizations, the United Nations is the least expensive option by far.

A study by the US Government Accountability Office estimated that it would have cost the United States approximately twice as much as the United Nations to conduct a peacekeeping operation similar to the United Nations Stabilization Mission in Haiti (MINUSTAH)—$876 million, compared to the United Nations budget of $428 million, for the first 14 months of the mission.

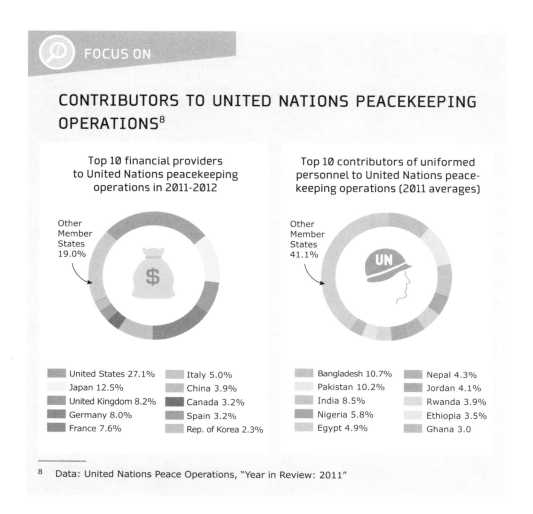

FOCUS ON

CONTRIBUTORS TO UNITED NATIONS PEACEKEEPING OPERATIONS[8]

Top 10 financial providers to United Nations peacekeeping operations in 2011-2012

Other Member States 19.0%

Top 10 contributors of uniformed personnel to United Nations peacekeeping operations (2011 averages)

Other Member States 41.1%

- United States 27.1%
- Japan 12.5%
- United Kingdom 8.2%
- Germany 8.0%
- France 7.6%
- Italy 5.0%
- China 3.9%
- Canada 3.2%
- Spain 3.2%
- Rep. of Korea 2.3%

- Bangladesh 10.7%
- Pakistan 10.2%
- India 8.5%
- Nigeria 5.8%
- Egypt 4.9%
- Nepal 4.3%
- Jordan 4.1%
- Rwanda 3.9%
- Ethiopia 3.5%
- Ghana 3.0

8 Data: United Nations Peace Operations, "Year in Review: 2011"

FINANCING THE UNITED NATIONS PEACEKEEPING MISSIONS

The United Nations peacekeeping budget is funded by Member states.

FIRST UNITED NATIONS PEACEKEEPING OPERATION

In November 1947, the United Nations General Assembly endorsed a plan for the partition of Palestine, providing for the creation of an Arab State and a Jewish State, with Jerusalem to be placed under international control. Palestinian Arabs and Arab States refused to accept the plan. On 14 May 1948, the United Kingdom relinquished its mandate over Palestine, and the State of Israel was proclaimed. The next day, the Palestinian Arabs and Arab States began fighting against Israel.

Shortly thereafter, the Security Council called for a cessation of hostilities in Palestine and decided that the truce should be supervised by the UN Mediator, with the assistance of a group of military observers. The first group of military observers, which has become known as the United Nations Truce Supervision Organization (UNTSO), arrived in the region in June 1948. In August 1949, the Security Council assigned new functions to UNTSO in line with the armistice agreements between Israel and its four neighbouring Arab countries—Egypt, Jordan, Lebanon and the Syrian Arab Republic. UNTSO's activities thus were spread throughout five States in the region.

UNTSO is the first-ever United Nations peacekeeping operation, and also the one with the longest history: to this day, its military observers remain in the region to monitor ceasefires and supervise agreements.

RECENT UNITED NATIONS PEACEKEEPING OPERATIONS

In the first 40 years of its history (1945-1985), the United Nations established 13 peacekeeping operations. Since then, 53 peacekeeping missions have been deployed.

United Nations Mission in the Republic of South Sudan (UNMISS)

The Security Council voted unanimously to establish a new mission in South Sudan on 8 July 2011, the eve of the country's independence. UNMISS has an authorized budget for up to 7,000 military personnel and 900 police personnel, as well as a civilian component. The new mission took over from the old United Nations Mission in Sudan (UNMIS), which was created following the signing of the 2005 Comprehensive Peace Agreement (CPA) that ended the Sudanese north-south civil war and paved the way for the independence of South Sudan.

The mandate of UNMISS is to consolidate peace and security and help establish conditions for development. The mission aims to strengthen the capacity of the Government of the Republic of South Sudan to rule effectively and democratically and establish good relations with its neighbours.

United Nations-African Union Mission in Darfur (UNAMID)

The Security Council authorized a joint African Union/United Nations hybrid operation in Darfur (UNAMID) on 31 July 2007. The Council commissioned UNAMID to take necessary action to support the implementation of the Darfur Peace Agreement, as well as to protect the country's civilian populations. The Council decided that UNAMID would start implementing its mandated tasks no later than 31 December 2007.

Free and fair elections taking place under the supervision of the UN in Timor-Leste.

United Nations Integrated Mission in Timor-Leste (UNMIT)

The United Nations was called in to East Timor (now Timor-Leste) in late 1999 to guide the Timorese towards statehood. This action came in the wake of violence and devastation after an earlier United Nations-led consultation on independence from Indonesia. Once there, UNMIT established an effective administration, enabled refugees to return to the newly independent country, helped develop civil and social services, ensured humanitarian assistance, supported the building of self-governance and helped establish conditions for sustainable development.

In 2005, the peacekeeping mission was transformed into an assistance and peace-building mission.

United Nations Stabilization Mission in Haiti (MINUSTAH)

The United Nations Stabilization Mission in Haiti (MINUSTAH) was established on 1 June 2004. It succeeded a Multinational Interim Force (MIF) authorized by the Security Council in February 2004, after an armed conflict that spread to several cities across the country caused President Jean-Bertrand Aristide to leave Haiti for exile. MINUSTAH's original mandate was to restore a secure and stable environment, promote the political process, strengthen Haiti's governmental institutions and promote and protect human rights.

The devastating earthquake of 12 January 2010, which resulted in more than 220,000 deaths, including those of 102 United Nations personnel, delivered a severe blow to the country's already shaky economy and infrastructure.

That year the Security Council increased the overall force levels of MINUSTAH twice in order to support the immediate recovery, reconstruction and stability efforts in the country. The Council also recognized the need for MINUSTAH to assist the Government of Haiti in providing adequate protection for the population and requested that MINUSTAH continue collaborating with the United Nations Office for the Coordination of Humanitarian Affairs (OCHA) and the United Nations Country Team on humanitarian and recovery efforts.

United Nations Mission in Sierra Leone (UNAMSIL)

The efforts of the international community to end an 11-year civil war in Sierra Leone and move the country towards peace have greatly improved the security of the environment there since 2002. After a decisive intervention by British troops in 2001, the United Nations helped disarm and demobilize some 75,000 combatants in the West African country. United Nations peacekeepers reconstructed roads; renovated and built schools, houses of worship and clinics; and initiated agricultural projects and welfare programmes.

 FOCUS ON

SIERRA LEONE AND "BLOOD DIAMONDS"

Diamonds from Sierra Leone and certain other African countries have become known as "blood diamonds" or "conflict diamonds."

In the 1990s, approximately $125 million worth of rough diamonds were bought in Europe. This staggering amount of money went to fund the anti-government forces that controlled the diamond mines and killed thousands of people during the civil war in Sierra Leone.

In response, the United Nations has implemented programmes to curb illegal diamond trading in Sierra Leone. One such programme is the Kimberly Process Certification Scheme, which "requires a paper trail that certifies the origin of rough diamonds." This will ultimately reduce the flow of "blood" or "conflict diamonds" from countries such as Sierra Leone and prevent the precious stones from being sold to fuel war crimes and crimes against humanity.

UNAMSIL, which drew to a close at the end of 2005, could serve as a prototype for the emphasis the United Nations now places on peacebuilding.

During its existence, UNAMSIL also helped Sierra Leone ensure the protection of the rights of its citizens; develop a professional and democratic police force; and bring to justice those who bore the greatest responsibility for violating international humanitarian law, through the United Nations-backed Special Court for Sierra Leone, which is currently still in operation.

The Security Council established a new mission—the United Nations Integrated Office for Sierra Leone (UNIOSIL)—to succeed UNAMSIL, with a mandate to help consolidate the peace, strengthen human rights, develop the economy, improve transparency and hold elections.

CREATING A SUSTAINABLE ENVIRONMENT FOR PEACE

The United Nations work for peace is not limited to the successful conclusion of a peacekeeping mission.

DO WE REALLY NEED THE UNITED NATIONS TO WORK FOR PEACE?

The world has witnessed more than 50 wars in the past 60 years. According to the Stockholm International Peace Research Institute, 15 major armed conflicts were waged around the world in 2010 alone. Luckily, none of them turned into a devastating world war. There is general agreement that the United Nations role in campaigning for peace and disarmament played a key role in this regard.

Many people feel that the United Nations should be made stronger so that it can stop smaller wars and carry out its decisions fully. But the effectiveness of United Nations actions depends on the political will of the Member States—on their readiness to respect and enforce the decisions they themselves take. Also, these operations require funding from States. Because of a lack of funds, the United Nations is often unable to play a greater role.

The strength of the United Nations comes from its refusal to give up, even in the face of the most difficult challenge. When countries at war do not have the political will to stop fighting, the United Nations must sometimes withdraw its peacekeeping troops; it continues its work, however, through diplomacy and negotiations, constantly speaking with the parties concerned. When conditions are better, the peacekeepers may return.

The world has a long way to go before it can ensure total peace and justice for everyone. Wars, poverty and human rights violations are still widespread. But that is precisely why we need the United Nations. Some say that if the United Nations didn't exist, the countries of the world would have to create another organization, maybe with another name, to do exactly what the United Nations does.

PEACEMAKING, PEACEBUILDING, PEACEKEEPING, NATION BUILDING

In the aftermath of a conflict, the United Nations helps displaced persons and refugees return to their homes. It clears mines, repairs roads and bridges and provides

FOCUS ON

THE PEACEBUILDING COMMISSION

The United Nations has played a vital role in reducing the level of conflict in several regions by mediating peace agreements and assisting in their implementation. However, some of those accords have failed to take hold, such as in Angola in 1993 and Rwanda in 1994. Roughly half of all countries that emerge from war lapse back into violence within a few years, driving home the message that, to prevent conflict, peace agreements must be implemented in a sustained manner over time.

In June 2006, the United Nations set up the Peacebuilding Commission, with a view towards helping countries transition from war to lasting peace. The Commission forms the connecting link between peacekeeping and post-conflict operations. Its job is to bring together all the major actors in a situation to discuss and decide on a long-term peacebuilding strategy. What that means is that assistance is better coordinated, money is better spent and there is real coordination between immediate post-conflict efforts and long-term recovery and development.

economic and technical help to rebuild the economy. It also monitors elections and closely follows how a country respects the human rights of its citizens. This process, also known as peacebuilding, has helped over 60 countries build democratic institutions. Peacebuilding provides all that is needed to support a country as it moves from war to peace and a functioning self-government.

Peacekeeping, as previously discussed, is organized around a military deployment. It is often a central part of the peacebuilding effort.

Nation building means different things to different people and is not a term used by the United Nations. It normally refers to a longer historical process that includes the creation of a national identity.

Peacemaking refers to the use of diplomacy to persuade parties in conflict to cease hostilities and negotiate a peaceful settlement of their dispute. All the types of action that can be used for preventive purposes, such as diplomatic peacekeeping, humanitarian aid and peacebuilding, have a role in creating conditions for successful peacemaking.

Some 300,000 children, boys and girls between the ages of 7 and 18 are involved in conflicts around the world.

CHILDREN AND ARMED CONFLICTS: VICTIMS OF CONFLICT

Children are unfortunately primary victims of armed conflicts. They are both its targets and increasingly its instruments.

Their suffering takes many forms during and after conflict. They are killed or maimed; orphaned; abducted; deprived of food, education and health care; often drugged; and left with deep emotional scars and trauma.

Boys and girls, some as young as seven years old, are recruited and used as child soldiers, forced to enact the hatred of adults. Girls face additional risks, particularly sexual violence and exploitation.

? DID YOU KNOW?

HIP-HOP ARTIST EMMANUEL JAL IS A FORMER CHILD SOLDIER

When Emmanuel was seven years old, he was recruited by the Sudan People's Liberation Army—one of thousands of children forcibly conscripted by the fighting forces. Many of those children did not survive. For nearly five years, Emmanuel was a child soldier who carried an AK-47 that was taller than he was. He was among thousands of young boys who fought the government forces by running through minefields. "Because we were lighter and could run fast, we had a better chance of surviving," he said.

Emmanuel, however, was lucky. When he was 13, he met an aid worker who took him to Kenya, where he was enrolled in school and found his way to a new life. "I was educated," he recalls. "It happened that I was helped."

For Emmanuel, education was an invitation to expand his identity, not trade it for a new one. "I feel a responsibility. I was once one of them, and I know a lot of child soldiers in the same position," he says.

Emmanuel uses hip-hop to spread a powerful message of peace and reconciliation. "Each album of mine always has a theme," he says. "'War Child' is about my story, my experience, what I have seen from the war and what I want to change. I want to make a difference."

"I survived to tell a story," he says. "I tell my story through the music. I want to inspire people."

Child soldiers

It is estimated that some 300,000 boys and girls under the age of 18 are involved today in conflicts around the world. Children are used as combatants, cooks, porters, messengers, spies, human mine detectors, sexual slaves, forced labourers and even suicide bombers. Physically vulnerable and easily intimidated, children typically make obedient soldiers. Many are abducted or recruited by force and often compelled to follow orders under threat of death. Others join armed groups out of desperation. As society breaks down during conflict, children lose access to school and are driven from their homes or separated from their families. Many perceive armed groups as

FOCUS ON

SPORT FOR DEVELOPMENT AND PEACE

Sport has historically played an important role in all societies, be it in the form of competitive sport, physical activity or play. But what does sport have to do with the United Nations?

Sport has a unique power to attract, mobilize and inspire. By its very nature, sport is about participation, about inclusion and citizenship. It stands for human values such as respect for the opponent, acceptance of binding rules, teamwork and fairness, all of which are principles also contained in the Charter of the United Nations. It is therefore not surprising that many United Nations Goodwill Ambassadors are internationally renowned sports players.

For the purposes of development, sport is defined broadly and encompasses all forms of physical activity that contribute to physical fitness, mental well-being and social interaction, such as play, recreation, organized or competitive sport, and indigenous sports and games. The focus is always on mass sport and not elite sport, because it's about more than individual development and promotion.

Sport also plays a significant role as a promoter of social integration and economic development in different geographical, cultural and political contexts. Sport can be a powerful tool for strengthening social ties and networks and promoting ideals of peace, fraternity, solidarity, non-violence, tolerance and justice.

Because of its properties of integration and post-trauma relief, and because it brings life back to normal for a while at least, the United Nations also uses sport to reach out to those most in need—refugees, child soldiers, victims of conflict and natural catastrophes, the impoverished, persons with disabilities, victims of racism, stigmatization and discrimination, persons living with HIV/AIDS, malaria and other diseases.

Liberian children participate in a Sport for Peace Programme.

their best chance for survival. Others seek to escape from poverty or join military forces to avenge family members who have been killed.

Collaborative efforts between the Office of the Special Representative of the Secretary-General for Children and Armed Conflict, the United Nations Children's Fund (UNICEF) and other key United Nations entities, as well as Member States, regional organizations, NGOs and civil society groups, have resulted in significant advances and tangible results for children.

Returning children to civilian life and hopefully to their families
UNICEF works to release children from armed forces and groups as soon as possible, even during conflict, and help them return to their families. As part of this, UNICEF supports services that care for the physical and mental health and well-being of such children, providing them with life skills and engaging them in positive activities oriented towards their future. These programmes adopt a community-based approach that includes support for other vulnerable children who have also been severely affected by the conflict, so as to promote reconciliation and avoid discrimination. These actions require a long-term perspective and a long-term commitment to both the children and the conflict-affected communities to which they return.

More than 100,000 children in over 15 countries affected by armed conflict have been released and reintegrated into their communities since 1998. In 2010 alone, UNICEF supported the reintegration of some 11,400 children formerly associated with armed forces and groups, along with 28,000 other vulnerable children affected by conflict.

A GLOBAL COUNTER-TERRORISM STRATEGY

"Whether we like it or not, our generation will go down in history as one that was challenged to protect the world from terrorism."
— *Ban Ki-moon,*
United Nations Secretary-General

The United Nations has long been active in the fight against international terrorism. Reflecting the determination of the world to eliminate this threat, the Organization and its agencies have developed a wide range of legal instruments that enable the international community to take action to suppress terrorism and bring those responsible for acts of terror to justice.

Sixteen international legal instruments have been negotiated through the UN dating back to 1963, including treaties against hostage taking, airplane hijacking, terrorist bombings and financing terrorism. A Security Council Counter-Terrorism Committee oversees how Member States carry out the commitments they promised after the attacks of 11 September 2001 and works to increase their capability to fight terrorism.

The United Nations General Assembly adopted a Global Counter-Terrorism Strategy on 8 September 2006. The Strategy—in the form of a resolution and an annexed plan of action—is a unique instrument that enhances national, regional and international efforts to counter terrorism. Its adoption marks the first time that all Member States have agreed on a common strategic and operational approach to fighting terrorism. Important new initiatives set forth include:

» Improving the efficiency of counter-terrorism technical cooperation, between countries so that all States can play their parts effectively.

» Putting in place systems to assist victims of terrorism and their families.

» Addressing the threat of bioterrorism by establishing a single comprehensive database on biological incidents, focusing on improving States' public health systems and acknowledging the need to bring together major stakeholders to ensure that biotechnological advances are not used for terrorist or other criminal purposes but for public good.

» Involving civil society, regional and subregional organizations in the fight against terrorism and developing partnerships with the private sector to prevent terrorist attacks on particularly vulnerable targets.

» Exploring innovative means to address the growing threat of terrorists' use of the Internet.

» Modernizing border and customs control systems and improving the security of travel documents, so as to prevent terrorists from travelling and stop the movement of dangerous and illicit materials.

» Enhancing cooperation to combat money-laundering and the financing of terrorism.

On 8 September 2010, the General Assembly conducted the second biennial review of the Global Counter-Terrorism Strategy. In a resolution adopted by consensus, Member States reiterated a strong and unequivocal condemnation of terrorism in all its forms and manifestations, "by whomever, wherever, and for whatever purposes". They also reaffirmed support for the Strategy's four pillars: tackling the conditions conducive to the spread of terrorism, preventing and combating terrorism, building the capacity of States to prevent and combat terrorism and strengthening the role of the United Nations System in that regard, and maintaining respect for human rights for all and the rule of law as the fundamental basis for the fight against terrorism.

Kofi Annan, then United Nations Secretary-General, visited Ground Zero a week after the terrorist attacks of 11 September 2001.

DISARMAMENT

Disarmament is often linked to weapons of mass destruction, such as nuclear warheads and chemical and biological weapons, but it goes further that that. In today's world, most of the arms used are small and light and can be wielded by an individual or a group of two or three people. Disarmament also comprises efforts to reduce the number of these smaller, and therefore more easily transportable, weapons.

THE IMPACT OF ARMED VIOLENCE

Armed violence—the intentional, threatened or actual use of weapons to inflict injury or death—takes many forms, from political to criminal to interpersonal, and appears in a wide range of contexts. Armed violence does not just happen in areas of conflict. It is widespread, and every region of the world is affected. It imposes a tremendous emotional and economic burden on individuals, families and communities worldwide.

Across all affected societies, young males, at the peak of their productive lives, are the most common perpetrators, as well as immediate victims, of armed attacks. Women, pre-adolescent boys and girls also suffer as both direct and indirect victims of armed violence.

It is estimated that roughly 750,000 people die each year as a result of the violence associated with armed conflicts and large- and small-scale criminality. Two thirds of these deaths occur outside war zones. In addition, as many as seven million people (about 10 times the number of those killed) are injured each year, with victims often suffering permanent disabilities and living with profound psychological as well as physical scars.

Armed violence not only destroys lives; it also has a negative effect on the economy, damaging infrastructure and property; limiting the delivery of public services; undermining investment in human, social and economic capital; and contributing to unproductive expenditures on security services. It is both a domestic and international security concern, because of trafficking and major population displacements. And let's not forget that it undermines development and constitutes an impediment to the achievement of the United Nations Millennium Development Goals.

The "Knotted Gun," a symbol of peace, is the creation of artist Karl Fredrik Reutersward, offered to the UN by the Government of Luxembourg.

CONTROLLING SMALL ARMS AND LIGHT WEAPONS

Small arms are not in themselves unlawful, and they have legitimate uses, including for national defence and the protection and safety of people and property by law enforcement officials. The value of their global trade, along with their ammunitions, is estimated at more than $7 billion per year. A prohibition is therefore not a solution. The problem lies with undocumented trade, which may run in the billions of dollars, as well as sale at very low cost or the dumping of ageing arms and surplus weapons in the arsenals of other countries. What we need is adequate regulation of their availability and use.

At a United Nations Conference on the Illicit Trade in Small Arms and Light Weapons in 2001, States agreed on measures to strengthen international cooperation in curbing this illegal arms trade. They unanimously adopted the United Nations

Programme of Action to Prevent, Combat and Eradicate the Illicit Trade in Small Arms and Light Weapons in All Its Aspects. The Programme, which is politically but not legally binding, contains a wide range of undertakings and actions that Member States have committed themselves to at the national, regional and global levels. These include developing, adopting and strengthening national legislation on small arms and light weapons; destroying weapons that are confiscated, seized or collected; and fostering international cooperation that allows States to identify and trace illicit arms and light weapons.

Between 1998 and 2008, the United Nations and associated entities collected more than 300,000 weapons and kept records of most of them. These records could help improve the understanding of the illicit arms trade and facilitate the monitoring of progress made by post-conflict countries as well as the efficacy of arms-reduction initiatives.

Because most steps taken so far towards controlling the trade and use of small arms and light weapons have not been legally binding, the United Nations will convene a Conference on the Arms Trade Treaty to elaborate a legal instrument that will regulate the transfer of conventional arms in the future.

ENSURING WORLD SAFETY BY REDUCING NUCLEAR WEAPONS

Humankind has avoided a nuclear war thanks in large part to the disarmament activities of the United Nations, in particular the push for the elimination of weapons of mass destruction. However, the world remains a dangerous place, as weapons supplies are still growing. More people train for war every day, and the costs of the arms race continue to escalate.

Consider this: In 1945, after two atomic bombs were dropped on Hiroshima and Nagasaki in Japan, the Second World War (1939-1945) came to an end. Since then, the world has witnessed many more wars. These conflicts have killed some 20 million people, more than 80 per cent of them civilians. Though nobody has used nuclear weapons again, there are now at least eight countries that possess nuclear weapons (nuclear powers). Despite big reductions, which occurred immediately after the end of the Cold War and the collapse of the Soviet Union, the total stockpile of nuclear weapons in the world now amounts to some 23,000 nuclear warheads, with a combined destructive capability of 150,000 Hiroshima-sized bombs.

In 1945, more than 120,000 people were killed in Hiroshima and Nagasaki (Japan) by atomic bombs. The Hiroshima Peace Memorial, the only structure left standing in the area where the first bomb exploded, became a UNESCO World Heritage site in 1996.

DISARMAMENT IS AN URGENT GLOBAL NEED

Now take a minute to count from 1 to 60, and then consider this: By the time you finish counting, the world has lost 25 to 30 children. During the same time, the world has spent about $3.1 million for military purposes.

Both the accumulation of arms and economic development require large-scale human and material resources. Since resources are limited, though, pursuing either process tends to happen at the expense of the other. There is growing agreement that, in the long run, the world can either continue the arms race or achieve social and economic development for the benefit of all, but it will not be able to do both.

General and complete disarmament—in other words, the gradual elimination of weapons of mass destruction—is one of the goals set by the United Nations. Its immediate objectives are to eliminate the danger of war, particularly nuclear war, and to implement measures to halt and reverse the arms race.

SOME UNITED NATIONS ACTIONS FOR DISARMAMENT

» The Partial Test-Ban Treaty, 1963, prohibits nuclear tests in the atmosphere, in outer space and underwater.

» The Non-Proliferation Treaty, 1968, prohibits the spread of nuclear weapons from nuclear to non-nuclear countries.

» The Chemical Weapons Convention, 1992, prohibits the use, manufacturing and stockpiling of such weapons.

» The Comprehensive Nuclear-Test-Ban Treaty, 1996, bans all underground nuclear test explosions.

» The Anti-Personnel Landmines Convention, 1997, prohibits the use, stockpiling, production and transfer of such mines.

» The Convention on Cluster Munitions, 2008, prohibits the use, stockpiling, production and transfer of such weapons.

» The new, bilateral Strategic Arms Reduction Treaty (New START), 2010, requires the United States and the Russian Federation to reduce their deployed strategic warheads to no more than 1,550 (each) in seven years.

An Iraqi girl learns about the danger of landmines thanks to the Mine Risk Education programme, funded by UNICEF.

MINE TERROR AND ACTION IN NUMBERS

» Number of countries affected by landmines and explosive remnants of war in 2009: 66 States and seven territories.

» Number of people estimated to have been killed or maimed by landmines in the last 30 years: over one million, of which 71 per cent were civilians and 32 per cent children.

» Number of new casualties in 2009: 4,000, down over 75 per cent from a high of 26,000 casualties in 1997.

» Land cleared of mine/ERW contamination in 2009: an area over five times the size of Paris, with 80 per cent occurring in Afghanistan, Cambodia, Croatia, Iraq, and Sri Lanka.

BATTLING CLUSTER MUNITIONS AND LANDMINES

Since the 1980s, the United Nations has been addressing the problems posed by millions of deadly landmines scattered in over 60 countries. Each year thousands of people—most of them children, women and the elderly—are maimed or killed by these "silent killers." Meanwhile, new landmines continue to be deployed in various countries around the world.

The United Nations Mine Action Service (UNMAS) acts as the focal point for mine action and coordinates all mine-related activities of United Nations agencies, funds and programmes. The work focuses on mine clearance, mine awareness, risk-reduction education, victim assistance and stockpile destruction.

Since the anti-personnel mine ban treaty went into force in 1999, the number of new victims each year has dropped, large tracts of land have been cleared, and the number of stockpiled mines has decreased by millions. The treaty has had a major impact on the global landmine problem. It has not, however, addressed another large problem: explosive remnants of war (ERW), which kill thousands of civilians annually. "Explosive remnants of war" refers to abandoned bombs and grenades but also cluster munitions, which fail to detonate but remain volatile and dangerous. United Nations-supported mine-action programmes help countries eliminate the threat of landmines and explosive remnants of war. An international movement seeking to limit the use of cluster munitions (weapons that contain and release many smaller explosive devices at the same time) has gained momentum in recent years.

NOBEL PEACE PRIZE

The Norwegian Nobel Committee decided to award the 2001 Nobel Peace Prize in equal portions to the United Nations and its Secretary-General, Kofi Annan, "for their work for a better organized and more peaceful world."

The Committee said the end of the Cold War had at last made it possible for the United Nations to perform more fully the part it was originally intended to play. The Organization was at the forefront of efforts to achieve peace and security in the world and central to international mobilization aimed at meeting the world's economic, social and environmental challenges. The Committee added that Secretary-General Annan had been preeminent in bringing new life to the Organization: "While clearly underlining the United Nations' traditional responsibility for peace and security, he has also emphasized its obligations with regard to human rights. He has risen to such new challenges as HIV/AIDS and international terrorism, and brought about more efficient utilization of the United Nations' modest resources."

The Secretary-General rings peace bell at UN Headquarters in New York to observe the International Day of Peace.

The Nobel Committee has honoured the United Nations System with the peace award 15 times so far:

2007: The United Nations Intergovernmental Panel on Climate Change (IPCC) and Al Gore, former Vice-President of the United States

2005: The International Atomic Energy Agency (IAEA) and Mohamed ElBaradei, IAEA Director General

2001: The United Nations and Kofi Annan, United Nations Secretary-General

1988: The United Nations Peacekeeping Forces

1981: The Office of the United Nations High Commissioner for Refugees (UNHCR) (second time)

1974: Seán MacBride, United Nations Commissioner for Namibia

1969: The International Labour Organization (ILO)

1965: The United Nations Children's Fund (UNICEF)

1961: Dag Hammarskjöld, United Nations Secretary-General

1957: Lester Bowles Pearson, Canadian statesman, for striving to end the Suez Crisis and Middle East question through the United Nations

1954: The Office of the United Nations High Commissioner for Refugees (UNHCR)

1951: Léon Jouhaux, a founder of the International Labour Organization

1950: Ralph Bunche, United Nations Trusteeship Director

1949: Lord John Boyd Orr, founding Director-General of the United Nations Food and Agricultural Organization (FAO)

1945: Cordell Hull, US Secretary of State and instrumental in establishing the United Nations

TEST YOUR KNOWLEDGE

1. How are poverty and conflict linked?

2. What work does the United Nations do for peace?

3. Who decides on the creation of a new peacekeeping mission?

4. Does the United Nations have its own army?

5. What are the two types of peacekeeping operations under United Nations command?

6. United Nations peacekeepers are easily recognized by what piece of clothing?

7. Can peacekeeping soldiers fight for one side of a dispute?

8. What is the cost of a year of peacekeeping versus the estimated military spending?

9. What does UNTSO stand for, and what do you know about it?

10. Define peacemaking, peacebuilding and peacekeeping.

11. What is the United Nations doing to combat terrorism?

12. In what country did the United Nations set up a mission in July 2011?

13. How do conflicts affect children?

14. Why are children drafted into armies?

15. How does sport help development and peace?

16. What United Nations office was established following the attacks of 11 September 2001?

17. Is disarmament important, and why?

18. Why is the destruction of small arms and light weapons crucial?

19. Why are mines such a threat?

20. How many times has the United Nations System been directly or indirectly awarded the Nobel Peace Prize?

CHAPTER 5

HUMAN RIGHTS

QUICK FACTS
ABOUT HUMAN RIGHTS

The Charter of the United Nations, which came into force on 24 October 1945, and the **Universal Declaration of Human Rights**, which was adopted in 1948, proclaim the equal rights of all men and women and of all nations, large and small.

_____

One of the great achievements of the United Nations is the creation of a large body of **human rights law**—a universal and internationally protected code to which all nations must subscribe and all people aspire.

_____

The **Convention on the Rights of the Child**, which entered into force in 1989, exists to protect and promote the rights of girls and boys everywhere in the world.

_____

The United Nations has defined a broad range of internationally accepted rights, including **civil, cultural, economic, political and social**. It has also established mechanisms to promote and protect these rights and to assist States in carrying out these responsibilities.

_____

United Nations legal instruments have banned the participation of **children under 18 in armed conflict** and prohibited the trafficking of children.

_____

In 2010, some 67 million school-age children were not in school, an overwhelming proportion of them in developing countries. Of the world's estimated 774 million **illiterate adults**, two thirds are women.

_____

In 2011, roughly 115 million children were still working with hazardous chemicals and pesticides in agriculture, with dangerous machinery or in mines. Millions of children were still forced into **bonded labour**, prostitution, pornography, armed conflict or other illicit activities.

_____

CHAPTER 5
HUMAN RIGHTS

HUMAN RIGHTS: WHAT ARE THEY?

> ALL human beings are born **free** and **equal** in dignity and rights.
> — *Article 1, Universal Declaration of Human Rights*

DEFINITION

Human rights are those rights that are essential for us to live as human beings. They are rights inherent to all people, regardless of race, colour, gender, language, religion, political or other opinion, national or social origin, property, birth or other status. Without human rights, we cannot fully develop and use our human qualities, our intelligence, talent and creativity.

Human Rights workers often travel to remote places to obtain or verify information.

All human rights—whether they are civil and political rights, such as the right to life, equality before the law and freedom of expression; economic, social and cultural rights, such as the rights to work, social security and education; or collective rights, such as the rights to development and self-determination—are indivisible, interrelated and interdependent. Without human rights, countries cannot fully develop their potential and therefore better standards of life will not be reached.

WHAT ARE OUR HUMAN RIGHTS?

All people have the right to:

>> life, liberty and security

>> freedom of expression

>> freedom from slavery

>> fair trial

>> equal treatment before the law

>> equal protection under the law

>> freedom from arbitrary arrest, detention and exile

>> freedom of movement

>> protection of private life

>> a nationality

>> freely contract a marriage and start a family

>> freedom of thought, conscience and religion

>> freedom of opinion

>> freedom of association

>> social security

>> work

>> equal pay for equal work

>> rest and leisure

>> a standard of living sufficient to guarantee health and well-being

>> education

>> take part in the cultural life of the community

>> protection of their intellectual property

CHARACTERISTICS OF HUMAN RIGHTS

Human rights are:

» **Universal** — They should be respected for all individuals across all boundaries and civilizations.

» **Inalienable** — They should not be taken away, except in specific situations and according to due process, as in the case of a person found guilty of a crime after a fair trial.

» **Interdependent and indivisible** — The improvement of one right facilitates advancement of the others. Likewise, the deprivation of one right adversely affects the others.

» **Equal and non-discriminatory** — The rights of all people should be respected, regardless of their race, colour, gender, language, religion, opinion, origin or status.

» **Both rights and obligations** — States assume the obligation under international law to respect, protect and fulfil human rights. At the individual level, we are entitled to our own human rights, and we must also respect the human rights of others.

THE UNITED NATIONS AND HUMAN RIGHTS

UNIVERSAL DECLARATION OF HUMAN RIGHTS

The idea of human rights did not begin with the establishment of the United Nations; its roots can be found across world cultures and religions. However, the adoption of the Universal Declaration of Human Rights by the United Nations General Assembly on 10 December 1948 was a landmark achievement in world history, as it was the first time that the international community set down formal standards of human rights and freedoms that should be enjoyed by everyone, everywhere.

The General Assembly then had called upon all Member States to publicize the text of the Declaration and "to cause it to be disseminated, displayed, read and expounded principally in schools and other educational institutions, without distinction based on the political status of countries or territories".

By this Declaration, governments accepted the obligation to ensure that all human beings—women and men, rich and poor, strong and weak, young and old, of all races and religions—are treated equally. The Declaration is not part of binding international law, but due to universal acceptance by countries around the world, it has gained immense moral weight and inspired both human rights development and a rich body of legally binding international human rights treaties.

DID YOU KNOW?

THE MOST TRANSLATED DOCUMENT IN THE WORLD

The Office of the High Commissioner for Human Rights has been awarded the Guinness World Record for having collected, translated and disseminated the Universal Declaration of Human Rights into more than 380 languages and dialects, from Abkhaz to Zulu. The Universal Declaration is thus the document most translated—indeed, the most universal—in the world.[9]

The United Nations has adopted a multitude of international human rights treaties and conventions, the most important of which are the two International Covenants—one on economic, social and cultural rights and the other on civil and political rights. The Universal Declaration of Human Rights, together with these two Covenants and their optional Protocols, are known as the International Bill of Human Rights.

---
[9]   All translations are available at *http://www.ohchr.org*

HUMAN RIGHTS LAW

The United Nations has been the driving force behind more than 80 human rights treaties and declarations for the rights of women, children, disabled persons, minorities, indigenous people and other more vulnerable groups. Together, these agreements have helped create a culture of human rights throughout the world, which has proved to be a powerful tool in curbing abuses and establishing a more just order for humankind, especially for the less powerful among us.

International human rights law lays down obligations that States are bound to respect. By becoming parties to international treaties, States agree to refrain from interfering with the enjoyment of human rights and to protect individuals and groups against

Eleanor Roosevelt, former first lady of the United States, was one of the authors of the Universal Declaration of Human Rights in 1948.

abuses. By ratifying treaties, governments commit to adopting national measures and legislation compatible with the terms laid out in the treaties. A country's domestic legal system therefore provides the principal legal protection of human rights guaranteed under international law.

When domestic legal proceedings fail to address human rights abuses, mechanisms for individual and group complaints are available at the regional and international levels. Under a confidential communications procedure, allegations of gross and systematic violations of human rights can also be submitted to the United Nations if domestic remedies have been exhausted and there is no possibility for obtaining justice in one's own country.

OTHER INTERNATIONAL HUMAN RIGHTS INSTRUMENTS[10]

> » Convention on Consent to Marriage, Minimum Age for Marriage and Registration of Marriages (1962)

> » International Convention on the Elimination of All Forms of Racial Discrimination (1965)

---

10 A complete list of international instruments can be found at *http://www2.ohchr.org/*

» Convention on the Elimination of All Forms of Discrimination against Women (1979)

» Convention against Torture and Other Cruel, Inhuman or Degrading Treatment or Punishment (1984)

» Convention on the Rights of the Child (1989)

» International Convention on the Protection of the Rights of All Migrant Workers and Members of their Families (1990)

» United Nations Principles for Older Persons (1991)

» Declaration of Commitment on HIV/AIDS (2001)

» International Convention for the Protection of All Persons from Enforced Disappearance (2006)

» Convention on the Rights of Persons with Disabilities (2006)

The legal status of these instruments varies. On the one hand, declarations, principles, guidelines, standard rules and recommendations have no binding legal effect, although they do have an undeniable moral force and provide practical guidance for governments. On the other hand, covenants, statutes, protocols and conventions are legally binding for those States that ratify or accede to them.

WHO IS RESPONSIBLE FOR HUMAN RIGHTS AT THE UNITED NATIONS?

Every United Nations body and agency is involved to some degree in the protection of human rights. However, the main United Nations group responsible for promoting and protecting human rights is the Human Rights Council.

Human Rights Council
The Human Rights Council was created in June 2006 to replace the Human Rights Commission, which had operated since 1946 but had been heavily criticized for allowing countries with poor human rights records to be members.

Responsibilities

The Human Rights Council is the main United Nations forum for dialogue and cooperation on human rights. It is empowered to prevent abuses, inequity and discrimination, protect the most vulnerable people and groups and expose perpetrators all around the world.

Human Rights Council and the General Assembly

As a subsidiary body of the General Assembly, the Human Rights Council monitors human rights situations in all countries and is directly accountable to the full membership of the United Nations. It is, however, administered by the United Nations High Commissioner for Human Rights.

The Human Rights Council is required to make recommendations to the General Assembly for further developing international law in the field of human rights and to undertake a Universal Periodic Review of each State's fulfilment of its human rights obligations and commitments. The Council has the authority to recommend that the General Assembly suspend the rights and privileges of any Member State in the Council that has persistently committed gross and systematic violations of human rights. This process of suspension requires a two-thirds majority vote by the General Assembly.

The Human Rights Council chamber in Geneva.

Composition and meetings

The Human Rights Council meets in Geneva for 10 weeks every year. It is composed of 47 elected United Nations Member States, each of which serves for an initial period of three years and cannot be elected for more than two consecutive terms.

High Commissioner for Human Rights

The High Commissioner is the principal United Nations official responsible for human rights. He or she reports directly to the Secretary-General.

The Office of the High Commissioner for Human Rights (OHCHR) leads global human rights efforts and represents the world's commitment to the universal ideals of human rights. It denounces violations worldwide, provides a forum for identifying, highlighting and responding to human rights challenges and acts as the principal focal point of human rights research, education, information and advocacy in the United Nations System.

OHCHR provides assistance—often expertise and technical training in the administration of justice, legislative reform, and the electoral process—to governments, civil society and other United Nations entities and organizations, in order to help them implement international human rights standards on the ground. The Office also assists the Human Rights Council and the committees that monitor the implementation of the core human rights treaties, which may call upon governments to respond to allegations of human rights violations (these committees are referred to as the Treaty Bodies).

Special rapporteurs and working groups

Special rapporteurs and working groups on human rights investigate violations and intervene in individual cases and emergency situations; these are referred to as "special procedures." United Nation human rights experts are independent. They serve in their positions for a maximum of six years and do not get paid for their work. The number of such experts has grown steadily over the years; at the end of 2011, there were 33 of them. They are assigned to report either on a specific country or territory (there were nine such cases in 2011) or on a theme (for example, right to food, violence against women).

In preparing their reports for the Human Rights Council and the General Assembly, these experts use all reliable resources, including individual complaints and information from NGOs. They may also initiate "urgent-action procedures" to intercede with governments at the highest level. A significant portion of their research is done in the field, where they meet with authorities and victims and gather on-site evidence of alleged violations and misconduct. Their reports are made public, thus helping to advertise abuses and emphasize the responsibility of governments for the protection of human rights. Apart from a few exceptions, governments do not like to be named and shamed and have rarely refused to let these investigating experts into their countries, for fear of a public outcry and tacit recognition of guilt.

International Criminal Court

In 1998, at a conference in Rome, 120 nations established a permanent International Criminal Court (ICC). In creating the Court, the world made it clear that impunity— exemption from punishment—is no longer acceptable. This Court, which came into being in 2002 when its founding treaty (the Rome Statute) came into force, prosecutes individuals for the most serious crimes, such as genocide, war crimes and crimes against humanity. As of September 2012, 121 countries were parties to the International Criminal Court.

The International Criminal Court is independent from the United Nations; however, the Security Council may refer human rights situations to the Court. For example, in 2005, acting on reports of widespread abuses, the Security Council referred the situation in the Darfur region of Sudan to the Court.

A real need exists for such a court. In countries at war, there may be no judicial system capable of dealing with war crimes. Those in power may also be unwilling to prosecute their own citizens for wrongdoing, especially if they are high-ranking. The International Criminal Court provides a just option in such cases, breaking the cycle of impunity.

Other international courts and tribunals

Over the past two decades, the Security Council has established, as subsidiary organs, two ad hoc, territorially specific, international criminal tribunals to prosecute crimes against humanity in the former Yugoslavia and in Rwanda. There are also three hybrid courts established respectively by Cambodia, Lebanon and Sierra Leone, with substantial help from the United Nations. These are not permanent and will cease to exist once their activities draw to a close.

» The Security Council established the **International Criminal Tribunal for the former Yugoslavia** in 1993, following massive violations of humanitarian law during the fighting in the former Yugoslavia. It was the first war-crimes court created by the United Nations and the first international war-crimes tribunal since the Nuremberg and Tokyo tribunals at the end of the Second World War. The Tribunal tries those individuals most responsible for appalling acts, such as murder, torture, rape, enslavement, destruction of property and other violent crimes. It aims to render justice to thousands of victims and their families, thus contributing to a lasting peace in the area. As of the end of 2011, the Tribunal had indicted 161 people.

» The Security Council created the **International Criminal Tribunal for Rwanda** in 1994 to prosecute those responsible for genocide and other serious violations of international humanitarian law committed in Rwanda between 1 January and 31 December 1994. It may also deal with the prosecution of Rwandan citizens who committed acts of genocide and other such violations of international law in the territory of neighbouring States during

 FOCUS ON

THE RWANDA GENOCIDE AND THE UNITED NATIONS

In 1994, Rwanda's population of seven million was composed of three ethnic groups: Hutus (approximately 85 per cent), Tutsis (14 per cent) and Twas (1 per cent). In 1993-1994, extremist elements of the Hutu majority, while telling the international community they wanted peace, were in fact planning a campaign to exterminate Tutsis and moderate Hutus.

During the 1994 genocide in Rwanda, up to one million people perished and as many as 250,000 women were raped. The killings shocked the world and left the country's population traumatized, its infrastructure decimated. If the absence of a resolute commitment to reconciliation by some of the Rwandan parties was one problem, the faltering response of the international community was another.

Since then, however, Rwanda has embarked on an ambitious justice and reconciliation process with the ultimate aim of all Rwandans once again living side by side in peace.

In 2005, the United Nations created an outreach programme of remembrance and education. The goals are to mobilize the international community, help prevent future acts of genocide and raise awareness of the lasting impact of the Rwandan genocide on survivors, particularly widows, orphans and victims of sexual violence, and the challenges they still face today.

the same period. In 1998 the Rwanda Tribunal handed down the first-ever verdict by an international court on the crime of genocide, as well as the first-ever sentence for that crime.

» The **Special Court for Sierra Leone** was set up jointly by the Government of Sierra Leone and the United Nations. It prosecutes those who bear the greatest responsibility for serious violations of international humanitarian and Sierra Leonean law committed in that West African nation since 30 November 1996.

» The **Extraordinary Chambers in the Courts of Cambodia for the Prosecution of Crimes Committed during the Period of Democratic Kampuchea** were created jointly by the Government of Cambodia and the United Nations, but are independent of both of them. The Cambodian court, with international participation, tries significant crimes committed during the Khmer Rouge regime (1975-1979), which killed up to three million people.

» The **Special Tribunal for Lebanon** prosecutes those who bear responsibility for the terrorist attack of 14 February 2005 in the Lebanese capital Beirut, which resulted in the death of Lebanese Prime Minister Rafiq Hariri and the death or injury of many others.

The Extraordinary Chambers of the Courts of Cambodia in session.

Mongolian farmers benefit from a project managed by the United Nations Development Programme, which helps them convert unused land into an agricultural park.

THE RIGHT TO DEVELOPMENT FOR ALL

DEVELOPMENT AS A RIGHT

The right to development is at the very heart of the United Nations efforts to promote and protect human rights. It is the focus of the 1986 Declaration on the Right to Development and is also highlighted in several other documents, including the 1992 Rio Declaration on Environment and Development and the 2000 Millennium Declaration.

DECLARATION ON THE RIGHT TO DEVELOPMENT

Development is a human right. Widening poverty gaps, food shortages, climate change, economic crises, armed conflicts, rising unemployment, popular uprisings, corruption of elites and other pressing challenges confront our world today. To respond effectively, the United Nations adopted the Declaration on the Right to Development, which unequivocally establishes development as a right and puts people at the centre of the development process.

The Declaration states that everyone is "entitled to participate in, contribute to, and enjoy economic, social, cultural and political development, in which all human rights and fundamental freedoms can be fully realized". Yet today, 25 years later, many children, women and men still live in dire need; their entitlement to a life of dignity, freedom and equal opportunity remains unfulfilled. This directly affects the realization of a wide range of civil, cultural, economic, political and social rights.

The pursuit of economic growth is not an end in itself. The Declaration clearly states that development is an all-encompassing process aiming to improve "the well-being of the entire population and of all individuals on the basis of their active, free and meaningful participation in development and in the fair distribution" of the resulting benefits.

Like all human rights, the right to development belongs to all individuals and peoples, everywhere, without discrimination and with their participation. The Declaration recognizes the right to self-determination and full sovereignty over natural wealth and resources. The right to development is not about charity; it's about enabling and empowering all women, men and children in their own countries to manage their own resources.

A FRAMEWORK TO PROMOTE ALL HUMAN RIGHTS

Because the right to development comprises all human rights—civil, cultural, economic, political and social, it provides a complete framework for the policies and

THE DECLARATION ON THE RIGHT TO DEVELOPMENT: WHAT IT SAYS

"The right to development is an inalienable human right by virtue of which every human person and all peoples are entitled to participate in, contribute to, and enjoy economic, social, cultural and political development, in which all human rights and fundamental freedoms can be fully realized." (Article 1.1)

"The human right to development also implies the full realization of the right of peoples to self-determination, which includes, subject to the relevant provisions of both International Covenants on Human Rights, the exercise of their inalienable right to full sovereignty over all their natural wealth and resources." (Article 1.2)

programmes of all relevant actors in the promotion and protection of human rights at the global, regional, subregional and national levels. The right to development:

» integrates aspects of both human rights and development theory and practice

» encompasses all human rights—civil, cultural, economic, political and social

» requires active, free and meaningful participation by all

» involves both national and international dimensions of State responsibilities, including the creation of favourable conditions for development and human rights

» demands that human beings be placed at the centre of development policy, that they be active participants and that they be guaranteed social justice and equity

» embodies the human rights principles of equality, non-discrimination, participation, transparency and accountability, as well as international cooperation in an integrated manner

» implies the principles of self-determination and full sovereignty over natural wealth and resources

» facilitates a holistic approach to the issue of poverty by addressing its root causes

» strengthens the advancement of the poorest people with due attention to the rights of the most marginalized

» fosters friendly relations between countries, international solidarity and cooperation and assistance in areas of concern to developing countries

The United Nations High Commissioner for Human Rights, Navanethem Pillay, said on 24 February 2011, of the uprising in the Arab world: "There is no doubt that the denial of people's right to development is one of the root causes fuelling public discontent and popular uprisings. [...] Then and now, still, people are taking to the streets because of rampant poverty and inequalities, rising unemployment, a lack of opportunities, and the chronic denial of their economic, social and cultural rights, as well as civil and political rights. They have no regular channels to express their discontent; they are deprived of the benefits arising from the natural resources of their countries, and they cannot meaningfully participate in the decision-making process to change the situation."

FOCUS ON

FORCED LABOUR AND HUMAN TRAFFICKING

One of the worse violations of human rights today is human trafficking—a crime that strips people of their rights, ruins their dreams and robs them of their dignity. It feeds off poverty and despair and physically and emotionally harms millions of men, women, boys and girls. Human trafficking is a global problem; no country is immune. It shames us all.

Today, at least 12.3 million people around the world are trapped in forced labour, including debt bondage, human trafficking and other forms of modern slavery. The victims are the most vulnerable people—women and girls forced into prostitution, migrants trapped in debt bondage, sweatshop or farm workers kept there by illegal tactics and paid little or nothing.

A few frightening facts[11]:

» The most common form of human trafficking (79 per cent) is sexual exploitation.

» The victims of sexual exploitation are predominantly women and girls: they account for about 80 per cent of the detected victims.

» In Eastern Europe and Central Asia, women are increasingly trafficking other women; shockingly, former victims become traffickers.

» Worldwide, almost 20 per cent of all trafficking victims are children. However, in some parts of Africa and Southeast Asia, children are the majority (up to 100 per cent in parts of West Africa). Child trafficking has been detected in all regions of the world.

» Forced labour accounts for at least 18 per cent of the detected victims, although this may be a misrepresentation because forced labour is less frequently detected and reported than trafficking for sexual exploitation.

» The United Nations estimates the total market value of illicit human trafficking somewhere between $32 and $52 billion a year.

» It is estimated that $28 billion is extracted every year from the victims of trafficking.

Unfortunately, human trafficking is nothing new. The transatlantic slave trade, which lasted some 400 years, marked one of the darkest chapters in human history. Ignorance or concealment of major historical events such as slavery constitutes an obstacle to mutual understanding, reconciliation and cooperation among peoples.

---

[11] United Nations Office on United Nations Office on Drugs and Crime (UNODC), Global Report on Trafficking in Persons (2009)

Rule of law

The concept of rule of law implies a system of governance based on non-arbitrary rules, as opposed to one based on the power and whims of a dictator. It is linked to the principles of justice and equity, involving ideals of accountability and fairness in the protection and vindication of human rights and the prevention and punishment of wrongs.

The United Nations supports the development, promotion and implementation of international norms and standards in most fields of international law. It also promotes the establishment of a rule of law at the national level that includes:

» a Constitution or its equivalent, as the highest law of the land

» a clear and consistent legal system

» strong institutions of justice, governance, security and human rights that are well structured, funded, trained and equipped

» transitional justice processes and mechanisms

» a public and civil society that is able to hold government officials and institutions accountable

These are the norms, policies, institutions and processes that form the core of a society in which individuals feel safe and secure. The challenge is to develop a system that is

FOCUS ON

HELPING THE VICTIMS OF TORTURE

Torture by the State is still practiced in many countries. The United Nations wants this to stop.

In 1984, the United Nations adopted the *Convention against Torture*. A 10-member Committee against Torture periodically examines reports from countries that have ratified the Convention.

Torture is strictly banned but still perpetrated in some countries. Men, women and even children continue to be tortured in detention simply for expressing their views, in order to force confessions or just because they were in the wrong place at the wrong time. The United Nations has also set up a Voluntary Fund for Victims of Torture. It provides psychological, medical, social, legal and economic assistance to victims of torture and their children.

Public defenders fulfil a vital role in judicial systems worldwide, offering legal representation to those who cannot afford it.

responsive to the needs of ordinary citizens, including the poor, and that promotes development. The electoral and legislative branches must be strong, people must have access to justice and public administration and governments must deliver basic services to all those in need.

Fairness, equity and justice are essential. They promote peace, protect human rights and sustain progress for all.

In a country where the rule of law is observed, human rights are respected. The State develops laws to protect its people from those who would violate them, even if the violator is the State itself. The police, lawyers and judges must remain fair and independent. No one can be arrested without serious grounds, detained for long periods awaiting trial or in inhumane conditions.

The judicial and legal process should be transparent, and it most certainly should not include forced disappearances, torture, slavery or executions. Instead, it should offer health services, educational programmes and vocational trainings for prisoners so that, once freed, they have a chance to get on the right path and care for themselves and their families without committing subsequent offences.

A State governed by the rule of law should keep its people safe from corruption, organized crime, trafficking—in such products as illicit drugs, weapons, rare fauna, flora and ivory products, counterfeit goods, cultural artefacts and human beings—as well as cybercrime, like child pornography and internet bullying, and environmental crime. It also cooperates with others to fight the international war against terrorism. The United Nations offers guidance, support and training to assist States in establishing appropriate policies and institutions and enforcing the rule of law.

Active, free and meaningful participation

> "Democracy cannot be exported or imposed from abroad; it must
> be generated by the will of the people and nurtured by a strong and
> active civil society."

> — *Ban Ki-moon*
> *International Day of Democracy,*
> *15 September 2011*

The link between democracy and human rights is captured in Article 21(3) of the Universal Declaration of Human Rights, which states: "The will of the people shall be the basis of the authority of government; this will shall be expressed in periodic and genuine elections which shall be by universal and equal suffrage and shall be held by secret vote or by equivalent free voting procedures."

 FOCUS ON

FREEDOM OF EXPRESSION

Anti-blasphemy laws and defamation laws against public officials and Heads of State seriously restrict free speech. Some countries even regard blasphemy towards holy personages or the official religion as an offence punishable by death.

The extent to which freedom of opinion and expression can be restricted by a government is one of the most challenged and sensitive topics in international human rights law. Some countries in Africa, Asia and Europe continue to jail, torture and kill people who to speak out and express their views. The United Nations advocates for the protection of the right of all men, women and children to free expression.

Free elections are crucial for allowing all people to participate in making decisions that affect them.

Democracy is a universal value based on the freely expressed will of people to determine their own political, economic, social and cultural systems and to fully participate in all aspects of their lives. It is as much a process as a goal, and only with the complete support of the international community, national governing bodies, civil society and individuals can the ideal of democracy be made into a reality to be enjoyed by everyone, everywhere.

While democracies share common features, there is no single model. For example, the chief of government can be elected directly by the citizens of the country or indirectly by representatives of the country's districts (constituencies). Sometimes the President is both Head of State and Head of Government, but in other democracies the powers are split between a President and a Prime Minister.

What all democracies share and must respect is the freedom of their citizens and, most importantly for the democracy itself, the freedoms of expression, speech, association and the press, all essential for citizens to stay informed, make their voices heard and be able to vote according to their best interests. Also key to the survival of the democratic system are respect for human rights and the holding of periodic and genuine multiparty elections by universal suffrage, which means including all men and women of eligible voting age.

Democracy provides a natural environment for the protection and effective realization of human rights. A democratic system empowers people to make decisions about their government, their lives and their future. It also fosters the development of individuals and communities who feel they can work to better their lives and, on a larger scale, improve society.

Overcoming poverty

Poverty as a violation of human rights

Poverty and human rights are intrinsically linked. Being out of work and therefore out of income is, of course, the basic definition of poverty, but to really understand what the condition is, one must also take into account a myriad of social, cultural and political factors. Poverty is not only a deprivation of economic or material resources; it is a violation of human rights, too.

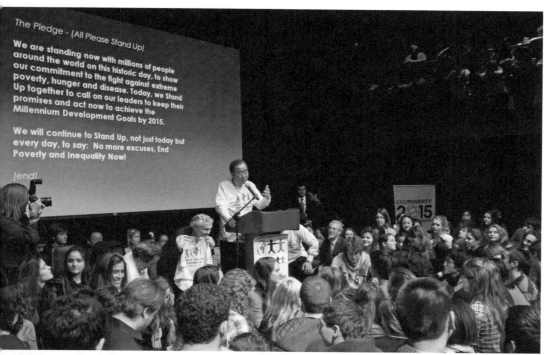

Secretary-General Ban Ki-moon stands before the "Stand Up Against Poverty Pledge" projected onto the wall at the United Nations International School (UNIS) in New York.

Being poor often means being deprived of economic and social rights such as the rights to health care, adequate housing, food and safe water, education and work. Poor people are locked in a vicious cycle: without work, they have no money, so they can't pay for health services and food; sick and malnourished adults can't go to work, and their children can't go to school; but without an education, these children will not find work either. The same is true of civil and political rights, such as the rights to a fair trial, political participation and security of the person. Poor people feel that they have no voice, that no one hears them.

The pursuit of human rights promotes the freedom, dignity and worth of every person—so, too, does the pursuit of human development. The fundamental recognition of the human rights dimension of poverty is reshaping the United Nations approach to the next generation of poverty reduction initiatives and policies. Attention is now given to the critical vulnerability and daily assaults on human dignity that accompany poverty.

Adding a human rights dimension to development programmes

To effectively eradicate poverty, the United Nations has added a human rights dimension to its development programmes. The pursuit of economic growth should not adversely affect the poor but, on the contrary, reinforce their ability to participate in the economic, political and social life of their societies by protecting their fundamental rights. Over the past decade, with this goal in mind, several countries have put in place or strengthened social protection initiatives to combat poverty. Even low-income countries can make significant progress on the Millennium Development Goals by establishing and implementing well-designed social protection initiatives.

The multiplying effect of gender issues

One way to make great strides against poverty and in the respect of human rights is to ensure gender equality. Poverty affects women and girls disproportionately: they are more at risk to be marginalized, isolated or victims of violence and trafficking. Numerous studies have shown a positive link between improvement in women's access to health care, education and other social benefits and economic growth, increased income and overall progress in a country's living standards.

Given that gender inequality helps perpetuate poverty, effective development strategies must take into account the protection of the full range of women's rights. The eradication of poverty must be based on sustained economic growth, social development, environmental protection and social justice, and it requires equal opportunities and the full involvement of women.

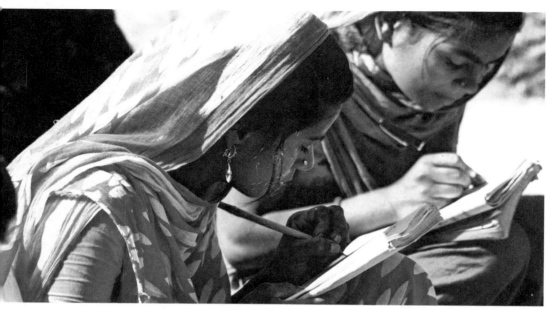

Educating women does not benefit just the students, but also their communities and society at large. A child born to an educated mother has much better chances of survival.

Fighting discrimination

The elimination of all forms of discrimination, including gender-based, is an overarching human rights principle that must guide the conduct of all States, big and small, developed or developing.

Combating discrimination against women

Gender equality is essential for the achievement of human rights for all, yet discriminatory laws against women persist in certain cultures. In some countries, laws continue to give women and girls second-class status with regard to nationality and citizenship, health, education, marital rights, employment rights, parental rights, inheritance and property rights. Such discrimination against women is incompatible with human rights.

Women form the majority of the world's poorest people, and the number of women living in rural poverty has increased by 50 per cent since 1975. Women labour for two thirds of the world's working hours and produce half of the world's food, yet they earn only 10 per cent of the world's income and own less than 1 per cent of the world's property.

Violence against women prevails on an unimaginable scale, and women's access to justice is often restricted. Discrimination based on gender and other factors, such as race, ethnicity, caste, disability, infection with HIV/AIDS or sexual orientation, further compounds the risk of economic hardship, exclusion and violence.

In some countries, women, unlike men, cannot dress as they like, drive, work at night, inherit property or give evidence in court. The majority of blatant discriminatory laws currently in force relate to family life, often limiting a woman's right to marry (or the right not to marry, in cases of early, forced marriages) or to divorce and remarry, thus allowing for sexually discriminatory marital practices like wife obedience and polygamy. Laws explicitly mandating "wife obedience" still govern marital relations in a number of countries.

FOCUS ON

THE UN WANTS TO END VIOLENCE AGAINST WOMEN

In 2008, United Nations Secretary-General Ban Ki-moon launched a campaign called "UNiTE to End Violence against Women." It aims to prevent and eliminate violence against women and girls in all parts of the world. The mission is simple: "Violence against women cannot be tolerated, in any form, in any context, in any circumstance, by any political leader or by any government."

For many years, women around the world have led efforts to prevent and end violence against their gender, and today more and more men are adding their support to the movement. Men have a crucial role to play, as fathers, friends, decision makers, and community and opinion leaders speaking out against violence against women and ensuring that priority attention is given to the problem. Importantly, men can also be positive role models for boys, offering healthy examples of masculinity.

The campaign calls on governments, civil society, women's organizations, young people, the private sector, the media and the entire United Nations System to join forces in addressing violence against women and girls.

By 2015, UNiTE aims to achieve the following five goals in all countries:

» adopt and enforce national laws to address and punish all forms of violence against women and girls

» adopt and implement multisectoral national action plans

» strengthen data collection on the prevalence of violence against women and girls

» increase public awareness and social mobilization

» address sexual violence in times of armed conflict

International human rights law, in particular the Convention on the Elimination of All Forms of Discrimination against Women, prohibits gender discrimination and includes guarantees for men and women to enjoy their civil, cultural, economic, political and social rights equally.

More than 30 years since the Convention's entry into force, the recognition and enjoyment of equal rights with men still remains elusive for large populations of women around the world. Over 180 States have ratified the Convention, yet some countries continue to discriminate against women in areas of personal and family life such as divorce, travel and education.

Combating discrimination against older people

The composition of the global population has changed dramatically in recent decades. Between 1950 and 2010 life expectancy worldwide rose from 46 to 68 years, and it is projected to increase to 81 by the end of the century. Almost 700 million people are now over the age of 60; by 2050, that number will reach two billion people, over 20 per cent of the global population and, for the first time in history, surpassing the number of children in the world. Human rights don't stop at 60!

Clearly we need to pay increased attention to the particular needs and challenges faced by older people. Just as important, however, are the essential contributions

Building a society for all ages is part of the United Nations action to promote human rights across the globe.

the majority of older men and women can continue to make to society if adequate guarantees are in place. Human rights lie at the core of all these efforts.

The Madrid International Plan of Action on Ageing and the Political Declaration adopted at the Second World Assembly on Ageing in April 2002 marked a turning point in how the world addresses the key challenge of "building a society for all ages". The Madrid Plan focuses on three priority areas: older persons and development, advancing health and well-being into old age and ensuring enabling and supportive environments. The Plan of Action is a resource for policymaking, suggesting ways for governments, non-governmental organizations and other actors to reorient the ways in which their societies perceive, interact with and care for older citizens. It represents the first time countries agreed to link questions of ageing to other frameworks for social and economic development and human rights.

Combating racial discrimination

Racial and ethnic discrimination occur on a daily basis, hindering progress for millions of people around the world. From denying individuals the basic principles of equality and non-discrimination to fuelling ethnic hatred that may lead to genocide, racism and intolerance destroy lives and communities. The struggle against racism is a matter of priority for the United Nations System.

The United Nations has been concerned with this issue since its founding, and the prohibition of racial discrimination is enshrined in all of the Organization's

FOCUS ON

CELEBRATING NELSON MANDELA

The elimination of South Africa's system of legalized racial discrimination, known as *apartheid* ("apart-ness" in the Afrikaans language), was on the United Nations agenda from its inception.

Condemning apartheid as a crime against humanity, the United Nations carried out a sustained campaign against it for more than three decades. It assisted in and supervised the country's first free and multiracial elections in 1994. Nelson Mandela, who was jailed under apartheid, became the first President of racially integrated South Africa.

Nelson Mandela International Day is celebrated by the United Nations every year on 18 July (Mandela's birthday).

core international human rights instruments. The United Nations tasks States with eradicating discrimination in the public and private spheres. The principle of equality also requires States to adopt special measures to eliminate conditions that cause or perpetuate racial discrimination.

In 2001, the World Conference against Racism produced the most authoritative and comprehensive programme for combating racism, racial discrimination, xenophobia and related intolerance: the Durban Declaration and Programme of Action. In April 2009, the Durban Review Conference examined global progress in overcoming racism and concluded that more remained to be achieved. The Conference renewed the world's commitment to an antiracism agenda.

Combating discrimination against minorities

Virtually all countries in the world have national, ethnic, linguistic and religious minorities within their borders. These groups and their members often face violations of their civil, cultural, economic, political and social rights on the basis of their defining characteristics.

Minority issues have been on the agenda of the United Nations for more than 60 years. Already in 1948 the General Assembly declared that the United Nations could

FOCUS ON

THE UNITED NATIONS AND THE HOLOCAUST

The Holocaust, which resulted in the murder of one third of the Jewish people along with countless members of other minorities, will forever be a warning to all people of the dangers of hatred, bigotry, racism and prejudice.

Rejecting any denial of the Holocaust as a historical event, either in full or in part, the United Nations General Assembly adopted by consensus a resolution condemning "without reserve" all manifestations of religious intolerance, incitement, harassment or violence against persons or communities based on ethnic origin or religious belief, whenever they occur.

The United Nations designated 27 January—the anniversary of the liberation of the Auschwitz Nazi death camp in 1945—as an annual International Day of Commemoration to honour the victims of the Holocaust. The Organization established an outreach programme, "The Holocaust and the United Nations," as well as measures to mobilize civil society for Holocaust remembrance and education, in order to help prevent the possibility of genocide occurring ever again.

not remain indifferent to the fate of minorities. The 2005 World Summit Outcome reaffirmed the importance of minority rights, stating that "the promotion and protection of the rights of persons belonging to national or ethnic, religious and linguistic minorities contribute to political and social stability and peace and enrich the cultural diversity and heritage of society".

The main point of reference for the rights of minorities is the United Nations Declaration on the Rights of Persons Belonging to National or Ethnic Religious and Linguistic Minorities (1992). It includes a list of rights to which people belonging to minority groups are entitled, including the right to enjoy their own culture, to profess and practice their own religion and to use their own language. The Declaration reaffirms that people belonging to minorities should enjoy all human rights and fundamental freedoms in accordance with the principles of non-discrimination and equality before the law. Other key ideas include the protection of the existence and promotion of identity and the right to effective participation.

Combating discrimination against indigenous peoples

The world's indigenous population is estimated at 370 million individuals living in more than 70 countries and is made up of more than 5,000 distinct peoples. Although they represent 5 per cent of the world's population, indigenous peoples account for

Indigenous peoples face many challenges in maintaining their identity, traditions and customs, and their cultural contributions are at times exploited and commercialized, with little or no recognition.

15 per cent of its poorest people. They face many challenges, and their human rights are frequently violated: They are denied control over their own development based on their own values, needs and priorities, and they are politically underrepresented and lack access to social and other services. They are often marginalized in discussions of projects affecting their lands and have been the victims of forced displacement as a result of ventures involving the exploitation of natural resources.

The United Nations has highlighted the problem of discrimination against indigenous peoples since the first Decade to Combat Racism and Racial Discrimination in 1973-1982. In December 2007, the General Assembly adopted the United Nations Declaration on the Indigenous Peoples, following more than two decades of negotiations between governments and indigenous peoples' representatives.

The Declaration is a key tool for the promotion and protection of the rights of indigenous peoples. It establishes a universal framework of minimum standards for their survival, dignity, well-being and rights. It addresses individual and collective rights, cultural rights and identity and rights to education, health, employment and language. It outlaws discrimination against indigenous peoples and promotes their full and effective participation in all matters that concern them. The Declaration also ensures their rights to remain distinct and pursue their own priorities in economic, social and cultural development.

Combating discrimination against migrants

The Durban Declaration, adopted by the World Conference against Racism in 2001, pointed out that xenophobia against non-nationals, in particular migrants, constitutes one of the main sources of contemporary racism. Migrants are often discriminated against in housing, education, health care, work and social security. This is a global issue affecting the countries of origin, countries of transit and countries of arrival. Around 200 million people live outside their countries of origin, which amounted to 3.1 per cent of the world population in 2010.

Migrants arriving illegally in a new country and victims of trafficking stopped by the police are often detained in administrative centres or prisons. Although the deprivation of liberty should be a last resort under international human rights law, migrants are often detained as a routine procedure and without proper judicial safeguards. Overcrowded immigration detention centres often have poor access to health care and inadequate food, sanitation or safe drinking water. There is also an increasing tendency to criminalize migration, which has, in too many cases, resulted in violations of migrants' rights.

Addressing negative perceptions of migrants within host communities is a key element of promoting their integration and enhancing their contribution to development. Various international instruments, in particular the International Convention on the Protection of the Rights of All Migrant Workers and Members of Their Families, address the issue of discrimination and provide guidance on human rights safeguards.

Combating discrimination against persons with disabilities

Over 650 million people around the world live with disabilities. In every region of the world, in every country, people with disabilities often live on the margins of society, deprived of some of life's fundamental experiences. They have little hope of going to school, getting a job, having their own home, starting a family and raising children, socializing or voting.

Persons with disabilities make up the world's largest and most disadvantaged minority. The numbers are damning: 20 per cent of the world's poorest people have disabilities, 98 per cent of children with disabilities in developing countries do not attend school, around a third of the world's street children live with disabilities and the literacy rate for adults with disabilities is as low as three per cent, one per cent for women with disabilities in some countries.

The Convention on the Rights of Persons with Disabilities is the international community's response to the long history of discrimination, exclusion and dehumanization of this marginalized group. A record number of countries have signed the Convention and its Protocol.

Players compete in a match for handicapped men at the national stadium in Port-au-Prince, Haiti.

CHILDREN HAVE RIGHTS, TOO

Human rights apply to all age groups: children have the same general rights as adults. But children are particularly vulnerable, and so they also have special rights that recognize their need for protection.

PROVIDING LEGAL PROTECTION FOR CHILDREN

Convention on the Rights of the Child

The Convention on the Rights of the Child sets out the rights that must be realized for children to develop their full potential, free from hunger and want, neglect and abuse. Children are neither the property of their parents nor are they helpless objects of charity. They are human beings with their own rights. The Convention offers a vision of the child as an individual and as a member of a family and community, with rights and responsibilities appropriate to his or her age and stage of development.

The Convention, a universally agreed-upon set of non-negotiable standards and obligations, has heightened recognition of the fundamental human dignity of children and the urgency of ensuring their well-being and development. It makes clear that an essential quality of life should be the right of all children, rather than a privilege enjoyed by only a few.

Children whose rights are respected are happier and healthier.

Optional Protocols to the Convention

In adopting the Convention, the international community recognized that people under 18 years of age often need special care and protection that adults do not. To help stem the growing abuse and exploitation of children worldwide, the General Assembly in 2000 adopted two Optional Protocols to the Convention, to increase the protection of children from involvement in armed conflicts and from sexual exploitation:

» The Optional Protocol on the involvement of children in armed conflict establishes 18 as the minimum age for compulsory recruitment and requires States to do everything they can to prevent individuals under the age of 18 from taking a direct part in hostilities.

» The Optional Protocol on the sale of children, child prostitution and child pornography draws special attention to the criminalization of these serious violations of children's rights. It aims to increase public awareness and cooperation between countries in efforts to combat them.

CHILDREN'S RIGHTS

Definition of a child

The Convention defines a child as a person below the age of 18, unless the laws of a particular country set the legal age for adulthood younger. The Committee on the Rights of the Child, the monitoring body for the Convention, has encouraged States to review the age of majority if it is set below 18 and to increase the level of protection for all children under 18.

DID YOU KNOW?

AN OPTIONAL PROTOCOL IS A TREATY RELATED TO A MAIN CONVENTION

Very often, human rights treaties such as the Convention on the Rights of the Child are followed by Optional Protocols, which may either provide procedures regarding the treaty in question or address a substantive area related to that treaty. Optional Protocols to human rights treaties are treaties in their own right, and are open to signature, accession or ratification by countries that are party to the main "parent" treaty.

Responsibilities and obligations

Parents, either natural or adoptive—or in some instances legal guardians, have the primary responsibility to provide for, protect and raise their children. However, governments of countries that have ratified the Convention are obligated to ensure that the children's rights are respected, protected and fulfilled. This involves assessing their social services and legal, health and educational systems, as well as levels of funding for these services. They must help families protect children's rights and create an environment where kids can grow and reach their potential. Governments should make the Convention known to adults and children. All adults, primarily parents and teachers, should help children learn about their rights, too.

What are children's rights?

Every child has the right to:

- » life
- » a legally registered name
- » a nationality
- » an identity (an official record of who they are)
- » care and guidance by both parents, unless they represent a threat to the well-being of the child, or if they become separated from the child, in which case a legal guardian assumes the parenting role
- » direct contact with both parents, in case of separation from one or both parents, except if it is contrary to the child's best interests
- » crossing borders to visit or be reunited with family living in other countries
- » protection from all forms of physical or mental violence, injury or abuse, neglect, maltreatment or exploitation, including sexual abuse, discrimination, abduction, sale and trafficking
- » appropriate protection and care (special attention must be given to the most vulnerable, like refugee children or those with disabilities)
- » freedom of speech, thought and religion
- » freedom of association
- » privacy
- » information (on his or her environment and rights, health issues and more)
- » participation in decisions affecting him or her

The first right of every child is the right to life. Parents or legal guardians have the primary responsibility to provide for, protect and raise their children.

» an adequate standard of living to meet physical and mental needs

» the best health care possible, safe drinking water, nutritious food and a clean and safe environment

» help from the government if he or she is poor or in need, particularly with regard to food, clothing and housing

» a primary education, which should be free, in order to develop each child's personality, talents and abilities to the fullest and to learn respect for peace and others' rights

» leisure, play and culture

» protection against work that is dangerous, inappropriate for children or that jeopardizes his or her other rights (health, education, leisure)

» a fair juvenile justice system, protecting detained children from abuse and treating them with dignity

» freedom from torture or cruel, inhuman or degrading treatment

» protection from the consequences of war and armed conflicts and especially from recruitment by armed forces

» rehabilitation if he or she has been neglected, abused or exploited, with special attention to restoring a child's health, self-respect and dignity

THE UNITED NATIONS AND CHILDREN'S RIGHTS

The United Nations and its agencies are involved at all levels in upholding and applying children's rights, offering a forum for States to discuss related issues as well as direct services for children on the ground and around the world.

From vaccination campaigns to provision of clean water and sanitation services, from the protection of child refugees to the rehabilitation of former child soldiers and victims of armed conflicts, the United Nations System is improving children's lives every day, working to make the world a better and safer place for them.

Education for All

The Education for All movement is a global commitment to providing quality basic education for all children, teenagers and adults. The movement was launched at the World Conference on Education for All in 1990. Ten years later, in 2000, with many countries far from having reached this goal, the international community met again in Dakar, Senegal, and reaffirmed its commitment to achieving Education for All by the

Offering a free meal to schoolchildren encourages enrolment and attendance, and increases students' learning capacity.

FOCUS ON

CHILDREN AND JUSTICE SYSTEMS

Over one million children are estimated to be detained worldwide. Most of them have not committed serious offences, and some have been jailed for their race, nationality or beliefs. In many cases children are detained for political reasons and have committed no crime at all.

Prison conditions in many countries, particularly those affected by conflict and crisis, are dire in terms of disease, sanitation and the need for water and food. Violence, especially against women and children, is widespread. The lack of access to education, health care or family members for long periods of time affects all prisoners, especially children. Inhumane conditions often lead to deaths, riots and other disturbances, and jeopardize the chances of a prisoner's social reintegration.

year 2015. The gathering identified six education goals that aim to meet the learning needs of children, teenagers and adults:

Expanding and improving comprehensive early childhood care and education, especially for the most vulnerable and disadvantaged children.

» Ensuring that by 2015 all children—particularly girls, children in difficult circumstances and those belonging to ethnic minorities—have access to, and complete, free and compulsory quality primary education.

» Ensuring that the learning needs of all young people and adults are met through equitable access to appropriate learning and life-skills programmes.

» Achieving a 50 per cent improvement in adult-literacy levels by 2015, especially for women, and equitable access to basic and continuing education for all adults.

» Eliminating gender disparities in primary and secondary education by 2005 and achieving gender equality in education by 2015, with a focus on ensuring girls' full and equal access to and achievement in basic education of good quality.

» Improving all aspects of the quality of education and ensuring excellence, so that recognized and measurable learning outcomes are achieved by everyone, especially in literacy, numeracy and essential life skills.

As the lead United Nations agency in this area, UNESCO is mobilizing and harmonizing the international efforts to reach education optimization for all.

In addition to solidifying the rights of children, the drive to achieve Education for All contributes to the global pursuit of the Millennium Development Goals, especially those on universal primary education and gender equality in education by 2015.

Sending girls to school

Thanks in part to the United Nations, today nearly 90 per cent of primary-school-age children are enrolled in school, a big jump from less than 50 per cent in 1960. This is great progress, but a lot remains to be done.

In some developing countries, girls were still facing discrimination in 2012. They often receive less food than boys do and are forced to work long hours, even when they are only five or six years old. In 2010, of the 68 million unenrolled primary-school-age children, 53 per cent were girls.

The Convention on the Rights of the Child requires governments to ensure that both girls and boys get an education. The obstacles that stand between girls and schooling are mainly due to poverty, armed conflict, cultural and religious values and geography.

Educating a girl dramatically reduces the chances that any children she has will die before age five. Furthermore, educated girls are likely to marry later and have fewer children, who in turn will be more likely to survive and better nourished and educated. Educated girls are more productive at home, better paid in the workplace and more able to participate in social, economic and political decision-making, which in turn makes countries and peoples more prosperous and developed.

Child labour

All over the world today, millions of children work to help their families in ways that are neither harmful nor exploitative. However, around 150 million children between the ages of 5 and 14 in developing countries—representing about 16 per cent of all children in this age group—are involved in child labour. An estimated 215 million children under 18 work, many full-time. Data show that in sub-Saharan Africa, 25 per cent of children between the ages of 5 and 17 work, compared to 12 per cent in Asia-Pacific and 10 per cent in Latin America.

Young boys learn carpentry skills to join the six per cent of children aged 5-14 years already working, according to the estimates provided by the United Nations Children's Fund.

Available numbers often indicate that more boys than girls are involved in child labour; however, girls are mostly involved in types of work that are invisible. For example, girls are thought to constitute 90 per cent of children involved in domestic labour. Even though the number of victims of child labour seems to have been decreasing in recent years in most parts of the world (except in Sub-Saharan Africa), too many children and teenagers are still suffering from it physically and mentally: working alters their development and interferes with their education.

Child labour is both a cause and a consequence of poverty. It harms the children, their families and their communities. It also prevents countries from making progress towards the Millennium Development Goals. Child labour is deeply linked to social inequities reinforced by discrimination. Children from indigenous groups, minorities, lower castes and of migrants are more likely to not attend school.

There has been considerable progress in the ratification of the International Labour Organization's (ILO) standards concerning child labour, namely of conventions on the worst forms of such labour and on minimum working age. However, a third of the world's children live in countries that have not yet ratified these conventions. Under the lead of the ILO, the United Nations is committed to achieving the elimination of the worst forms of child labour by 2016.

Fighting child selection

In 2011, the Office of the High Commissioner for Human Rights (OHCHR), the United Nations Population Fund (UNFPA), the United Nations Children Fund (UNICEF), UN-Women and the World Health Organization (WHO) joined forces against sex

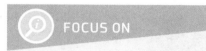 FOCUS ON

CHILDREN WHO WORK

Twelve-year-old Leandra Cristina Da Silva worked hard for a living. Instead of playing in her backyard or attending school, she laboured seven days a week, coated with dust and grime in the filth of the Olinda garbage dump on the out-skirts of Recife in northern Brazil. Although she lived close to the sea, Leandra had never seen the Atlantic Ocean. After finishing her chores at home, Leandra would leave every morning to work alongside her mother for 10 hours or more each day, scavenging for cans and bottles to sell. After an exhausting day at the dump, she would return to a home without running water and crawl into a bed that she shared with her mother and siblings.

The dump is dangerous. When the supermarket truck appears, men, women and children scramble to get the best garbage. Yet for all the drudgery and hazards, Leandra would barely earn the equivalent of $3 a day selling the collected bottles to a middleman, who makes money exploiting children. It is illegal for children in Brazil to work in such dangerous conditions, but poverty forces parents to take risks to feed their families. Since education is the best way to fight pov-erty, the United Nations Children's Fund (UNICEF) and the International Labour Organization joined forces with the Government of Brazil to help get children back in school. The Bolsa Escola ("School Scholarship") programme gives grants to families to replace the income children would bring in.

Leandra longed to go to school. Her mother, Marcia, had worked all her life and did not get any education. She did not really understand that the bolsa would replace the money her daughter earned at the dump to help support the family. But then, one day, with the help of UNICEF Project Officer Ana Maria Azevedo and UNICEF Goodwill Ambassador Susan Sarandon, Leandra was awarded a bolsa. She was thrilled to make a new start.

selection, a process favouring boys that takes place in parts of South, East and Central Asia. Ratios as high as 130 boys for every 100 girls have been observed. Sex selection is a symptom of social, cultural, political and economic injustices against women, and a manifest violation of human rights. "Women have to bear the consequences of giving birth to an unwanted girl child. These consequences can include violence, abandonment, divorce or even death," according to the United Nations agencies. Faced with such pressure, women often seek to discover the sex of a foetus through ultrasound, which can lead to abortion.

In some countries, prenatal sex determination and disclosure are illegal, while others have laws banning abortion for sex selection. But such restrictions are circumvented by the use of clandestine procedures, which may put women's health in jeopardy. In some areas, the lack of women has become so acute that it has led to an upsurge in their trafficking from other regions. States are obliged to act against these crimes and injustices.

All children, boys and girls, have the same rights.

TEST YOUR KNOWLEDGE

1. What are human rights?

2. Can you list some of the rights?

3. What are the characteristics of human rights?

4. Which United Nations body has primary responsibility for human rights?

5. Other than adopting international laws, how does the United Nations protect human rights?

6. What is the function of a special rapporteur?

7. Why is the right to development important?

8. What is the rule of law?

9. What do you know about the link between democracy and the protection of human rights?

10. What is the Holocaust?

11. What are some of the causes of genocide? Talk briefly about a recent act of genocide.

12. Who is most at risk of becoming a victim of human trafficking, and why?

13. What does the Declaration on the Rights of Indigenous Peoples say?

14. What does the United Nations do to promote and protect women's rights?

15. What group of people makes up the world's largest and most disadvantaged minority?

16. Why was the Convention on the Rights of the Child adopted?

17. Name at least five rights specific to children.

18. What rights does the Education for All movement seek to promote?

19. Why is child selection harmful to human rights and countries?

CHAPTER 6

HUMANITARIAN CRISES
AND RESPONSES

QUICK FACTS
ABOUT HUMANITARIAN CRISES
AND RESPONSES

When an event (or a series of events) critically threatens the health, safety, security or well-being of a large group of people, usually over a wide area, it is called a **humanitarian crisis or disaster**.

—————————————————

Armed conflicts, epidemics, famines, natural disasters and other emergencies may all involve or lead to humanitarian crises.

—————————————————

Nearly 90 per cent of natural disasters today are caused by **climate** and **water-related hazards**, such as floods, tropical storms and long periods of drought.

—————————————————

Every year, more than 200 million people are affected by **natural disasters**.

—————————————————

Altogether, well over 600,000 lives have been recently claimed by the 2004 Indian Ocean **tsunami**, the 2008 Nargis **cyclone** in Myanmar, the 2010 **earthquake** in Haiti and the 2011 earthquake and tsunami in Japan and **floods** in Thailand.

—————————————————

Currently, more than 43.3 million people are **forcibly displaced** worldwide.

—————————————————

There are 27.1 million internally displaced persons, 15.2 million **refugees** and 983,000 **asylum seekers** in the world today.

—————————————————

Nearly 80 per cent of the world's **refugees** are hosted by developing countries.

—————————————————

Most **armed conflicts** today happen within countries and not between countries.

—————————————————

CHAPTER 6
HUMANITARIAN CRISES AND RESPONSES

EMERGENCIES THAT AFFECT PEOPLE AROUND THE WORLD

DIFFERENT TYPES OF DISASTERS

Natural disasters

Every year, more than 200 million people are affected by natural disasters. Weather, climate and water-related hazards, such as floods, tropical storms and long periods of drought, account for nearly 90 per cent of natural disasters today. They destroy countless lives, leaving many people homeless and displaced. Sometimes they destroy livelihoods and community infrastructures, as when they render roads inaccessible and kill off resources necessary for the next harvest. Significant food shortage and the spread of infections and diseases can also create chronic crises and emergencies in the aftermath of a natural disaster.

Man-made disasters

Another type of disaster is human-caused, triggered by conflicts or civil wars. Man-made disasters uproot millions of people across the globe, leading to a wide range of emergencies, including food crises and massive displacement of populations. Victims of man-made disasters are usually forced to leave their homes and live on the edge, eking out an existence without the protection of their basic rights. During exile, many are exposed to violence, abuse or exploitation. They may have difficulty gaining access to facilities that secure safe water, as wells are often contaminated or mined by combatants during a conflict. Hunger and malnutrition, loss of safety and security and poor access to basic services, especially health care, are a few examples of hardships triggered by man-made disasters.

In Sri Lanka after the Indian Ocean Tsunami of 26 December 2004.

RECENT DISASTER TRENDS

In recent years, the trends in emergencies and crises have differed from the previous few decades, posing new threats and concerns to the world's population with highly complex and challenging issues. Those issues include a global food crisis, climate change and disease epidemics such as HIV/AIDS.

In addition, the magnitude and frequency of disasters vary, and multiple disasters can occur simultaneously. A recent trend shows a series of catastrophic natural and climate-related events that have required very high and sustained levels of humanitarian assistance from the international community and particularly from the United Nations.

RECENT DISASTERS ACROSS THE GLOBE

Recent figures from the United Nations International Strategy for Disaster Reduction (UNISDR) show floods claimed over 5,000 lives in 2011, while storms claimed over 3,000.

In addition, more than 45 per cent of the disasters that occurred in 2011 took place in Asia. Over 85 per cent of those killed and affected globally and 75 per cent of economic damages were also in Asia.

Middle East and North Africa (2011–2012)

»   The wave of political turmoil and change that swept the region in 2011 and 2012 caused widespread violence across Libya, Syria and Yemen, creating urgent humanitarian needs. In the first half of 2011, more than 900,000 people fled Libya, primarily to Egypt and Tunisia. By the summer of 2012, thousands of Syrians had fled their country, primarily to Turkey, Lebanon and Jordan.

Thailand (2011)

»   Severe floods hit the Thai capital, Bangkok, in October—the worst in five decades. They cost the country an estimated $40 billion. More than 1,000 factories were shut down, and 700,000 people were put out of work. Over 800 people died in the disaster.

Horn of Africa (2011)

»   By the middle of 2011, extreme hunger and famine were ravaging the Horn of Africa, affecting over 13 million people and killing tens of thousands of children in Somalia. Another 750,000 children were at imminent risk of death as of October 2011.

Pakistan (2011)

»   For the second year in a row, massive flooding affected more than five million people, forcing many from their homes and creating a deep food security crisis in the affected areas.

Japan (2011)

»   A 9.0 magnitude earthquake was followed by a tsunami and a subsequent nuclear power crisis, killing 15,500 people. The Fukushima Nuclear Power Plant was hit by the tsunami, resulting in the evacuation of nearly 2,800 local residents because of radiation leaks.

Haiti (January 2010)

»   A 7.0 magnitude earthquake almost completely destroyed the capital, Port-au-Prince, killing an estimated 220,000 people. More than 1.5 million others were left displaced and in need of food, water and medical supplies. The United Nations itself lost more than a hundred employees and contractors in the disaster.

THE IMPACT OF DISASTERS:
KEY HUMANITARIAN NEEDS AND RISK MANAGEMENT

Food

Food is our most basic human need, and it is also a human right. An empty stomach slows down physical and mental activities. With a lack of vital nutrients in the system, the hungry body has difficulty fighting against disease and infection. Today, hunger and malnutrition constitute the number one health risk worldwide, claiming millions of lives.

Shelter

The idea of shelter, or home, represents peace and comfort, protection and security. Home is a place where we live, play, eat, sleep and rest. People who lose their shelter and live in precarious conditions, with no access to basic needs, can experience severe stress and emotional discomfort. Having a home is vital for survival, which is why all human beings have the right to housing as part of an adequate standard of living.

Water, sanitation and hygiene

Lack of access to safe water and sanitation facilities, as well as poor hygienic practices, can cause major health problems. Dirty hands and dirty water allow viruses and bacteria to spread easily. Millions of people, especially children in developing countries, suffer from water- and sanitation-related diseases and infections, including diarrhoea, cholera, malaria, parasites and worm infestations. The right to live in healthy conditions is guaranteed under international standards.

Education

In school, children and adolescents learn academic, vocational and life skills. School provides a safe environment where they can play and interact with peers, reducing the possible risk of their exposure to violence. The right of children to benefit from education is also guaranteed under international standards.

COORDINATION OF EMERGENCY ASSISTANCE

Right help for the right people at the right time

For successful delivery of emergency relief action, it is crucial to have an accurate assessment of the situation at the onset of a crisis. This includes a breakdown of exactly what kind of humanitarian assistance is most needed, who will be the beneficiaries of such assistance, how long such aid will be provided for and what kind of logistical difficulties will most likely be encountered.

One of the largest airplanes in the world, the Ukrainian-designed Antonov 124-100 can carry a helicopter across the globe in minimal time. The helicopter is used for emergency relief operations, evacuations and other missions.

There are many actors involved in humanitarian action—the United Nations System, governments, non-governmental organizations (NGOs), civil society, local and international partners and many other relief agencies. Together they constitute the backbone of the international humanitarian community, working to feed the hungry, relieve the poor and provide shelter, protection and care to those who have lost their homes and family members. Only through an effective partnership and coordination among these actors is it possible to achieve success in humanitarian work.

INTER-AGENCY COORDINATION

As the Secretariat of the Inter-Agency Standing Committee (IASC) and of rapid-response teams, the United Nations Office for the Coordination of Humanitarian Affairs (OCHA) plays a crucial role in the immediate assessment of a humanitarian crisis and coordination of joint assistance. It can dispatch the United Nations Disaster Assessment and Coordination (UNDAC) team within 12-48 hours of a crisis anywhere in the world.

OCHA has adopted IASC's "cluster approach" in the coordination of programmes. This groups together United Nations and non-United Nations humanitarian agencies with a shared operational interest and divides field responsibilities among them. The "cluster approach" is effective in helping agencies avoid gaps and duplications in their humanitarian roles and undertake relief activities to the best of their capabilities.

In responding to disasters, the clusters cover a wide range of areas—agriculture, camp coordination and management, early recovery, emergency shelter, logistics, nutrition, water sanitation and hygiene, restoration of telecommunications, and more. As one example, the Office of the United Nations High Commissioner for Refugees/the United Nations Refugee Agency (UNHCR) is a global leader for emergency shelter cluster. When there is a massive influx of refugees or internally displaced persons (IDPs) in a region, UNHCR will put together all of the available assistance from many humanitarian partners and lead the relief action to provide refugees and IDPs with temporary shelter and other basic supplies.

Humanitarian workers risk their lives to improve those of others. They are the link to a better tomorrow for millions of people affected by disasters.

WHO ARE THE HUMANITARIAN WORKERS?

The humanitarian workers are doctors and surgeons, nurses, psychologists, teachers, photographers, journalists, TV and radio technicians, car and lorry drivers, plane and helicopter pilots, economists, auditors, jurists, press officers, translators and interpreters. They are experts in fields as diverse as agriculture, communication, human rights, climate change, water resource management, accounting, finance, logistics, disaster prevention, democratic governance, terrorism and engineering. They are specialists in nutrition, gender issues, multimedia, education, information technologies, sanitation services, police training, rebuilding of livelihoods, and post-traumatic therapy. They are administrators, coordinators, project managers, advisors, employees, consultants, volunteers and people from the local communities, all highly dedicated men and women from around the world.

Despite these many differences, they have a lot in common. Humanitarian workers dedicate themselves to assisting those in need, regardless of the recipients' race, religion or social status. They operate in places that are often remote, difficult and hostile. They risk their own lives to help others. Many have lost colleagues or loved ones as, over the years, humanitarian work has become more dangerous. The level of threats and number of deliberate attacks on aid organizations, including staff, equipment and facilities, has risen dramatically. In 2010, 242 aid workers were killed, injured or kidnapped.

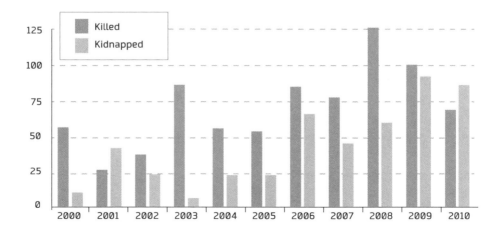

Humanitarian workers killed/kidnapped

Source: aidworkersecurity.org

Emergency food relief in North Kivu, Democratic Republic of the Congo.

UNITED NATIONS AGENCIES IN THE FIELD: WHO IS ON THE GROUND?

IMMEDIATE EMERGENCY RESPONSE: SAVING MORE LIVES

Immediate emergency response covers most crises that require instantaneous relief action, ranging from slow-onset hazards like droughts or crop failures to more complex disasters involving armed conflict or population displacement. In the field, United Nations agencies and many other humanitarian organizations work around the clock to meet the most critical needs during crises. Some high-profile emergencies require a concerted action involving various humanitarian bodies for a longer period of time, depending on scope and scale.

World Food Programme (WFP)

> » **What it does:** Feeds the hungry and poor.

> » **How it operates:** Establishes an emergency operation within 24 hours of a disaster outbreak to feed survivors.

The World Food Programme (WFP) procures locally produced food to cut down on transportation costs and help sustain local economies. Half of the food distributed by WFP is procured within the affected country or near crisis zones.

Food is given to the hungry at refugee camps, therapeutic feeding centres and other emergency shelters.

World Health Organization (WHO)

» **What it does:** Fights against outbreaks of emerging epidemic-prone diseases.

» **How it operates:** Distributes emergency vaccines and supplies for local health facilities during crises.

The World Health Organization (WHO) treats communicable diseases, including HIV/AIDS, tuberculosis, malaria, measles and influenza in affected communities.

DID YOU KNOW?

RECENT EXAMPLES OF FIELD ACTIONS

WFP provided immediate relief to victims of natural disasters

» In response to the 2010 Haiti earthquake, WFP delivered one million rations to more than 200,000 people in the week after the quake and fed four million people in six weeks. Following the 2010 Pakistan flood, it reached over three million people in the first month and 8.7 million in one year.

WHO launched a vaccination campaign in the Horn of Africa

» In July 2011, WHO provided vaccinations against polio and measles to an estimated 215,000 children in the affected areas of the Horn of Africa, the region's refugee camps and along the Somali-Kenyan border.

UNICEF is helping children all over the world

» In 2010, UNICEF responded to nearly 290 humanitarian situations in 98 countries, with the Supply Division supporting 69 countries in emergencies.

Recent UNHCR relief response

» During 2011, UNHCR provided protection or assistance to roughly 26 million people, including 10.5 million refugees and around 15 million internally displaced persons. During 2011, in Libya alone, well over one million people had left the country and more than 200,000 people became internally displaced within the country itself. UNHCR chartered 115 aircraft to evacuate third country nationals.

United Nations Children's Fund (UNICEF)

» **What it does**: Child survival and protection, development and education.

» **How it operates:** UNICEF's Supply Division can pack and ship essential emergency supplies and pre-packaged kits within 48 hours following a disaster.

UNICEF provides emergency immunization, vitamin A supplementation and other health services for children and their families. It also provides basic care services for HIV/AIDS and post-rape and psychosocial health training for community health-care workers.

For water, sanitation and hygiene crises, it rehabilitates water points and constructs hand-washing facilities and latrines.

It operates therapeutic feeding centres and supports local schools in reconstructing classrooms for children.

FOCUS ON

CHILDREN DURING CRISES

Children are especially vulnerable during emergencies. Each year, almost 11 million children die before reaching the age of five. More than two million children died from armed conflict in the last decade, and 20 million children were displaced worldwide, while nearly 300,000 under the age of 18 were recruited as war soldiers.

Children can easily become victims of:

» extreme poverty

» hunger and malnutrition, which weaken a child's learning ability and affect the immune system. When a woman suffers from malnutrition during pregnancy, her baby is at risk of being born with a low birth weight, which increases the risk of other health problems, disabilities or death

» infections or diseases: measles, diarrhoea, parasite or acute respiratory infections, malaria, HIV/AIDS

» severe injuries or death during emergencies

» unnecessary displacement or becoming orphaned during exile

» violence: abuse, exploitation, abduction, recruitment into armed conflict and sexual or gender-based violence (SGBV), including rape, prostitution, mutilation, forced pregnancy and sexual slavery

A mother and her child are repatriated from the Aramba IDP camp to their village home in Sehjanna, North Darfur.

Office of the United Nations High Commissioner for Refugees/ The United Nations Refugee Agency (UNHCR)

» **What it does:** Assists and protects forcibly displaced people.

» **Who it helps:** Refugees, asylum seekers, returnees, internally displaced people, stateless people and others in similar situations, children and women in particular. (Half of the 36.4 million people of concern to UNHCR are children.)

» **How it operates:** UNHCR can dispatch 300 skilled personnel in less than 72 hours following a crisis.

» UNHCR provides emergency shelter—refugee camps, collective centres, makeshift shelters—and essential goods, including tents, blankets and plastic sheeting.

» It helps build clinics, schools and water wells for shelter inhabitants and gives them access to health care and psychosocial support during their exile.

» It coordinates family reunification activities and demobilization, disarmament and integration programmes for children associated with armed forces.

FOCUS ON

DISPLACED MEN AND BOYS

In an effort to ensure the protection of women and girls, discussions about humanitarian assistance have sometimes neglected the situation of adult men and young boys. They, too, have particular needs, face difficult situations and fear for their lives, survival and freedom. When refugee movements are provoked by a human-made disaster, like armed conflict — rather than a natural catastrophe, such as flooding — men and boys are often more directly affected. They run the risk of being forcibly recruited into armies and militia groups.

LONG-TERM EMERGENCY RESPONSE: GETTING PEOPLE BACK ON THEIR FEET

From time to time, depending on the impact of a disaster or prolonged conflict, circumstances may require going beyond a one-time emergency response. In such cases, United Nations agencies, together with other humanitarian bodies, draw up long-term plans for recovery that entail complex and prolonged projects aiming to rebuild and develop the sustainability of crisis-ridden areas.

Key focus activities during long-term emergency responses are:

- » increasing food security through continuous food assistance and introduction of new agricultural practices

- » coordination of voluntary repatriation, resettlement or integration of refugees

- » improvement of health-care services and community interventions

- » securing safe water and improved sanitation facilities

- » support for the education of children and teenagers

United Nations Food and Agriculture Organization (FAO)

The United Nations Food and Agriculture Organization (FAO) aims to improve agricultural productivity in food-crisis regions. While continuing its food aid, it reaches out to rural populations in particular, in order to help them rehabilitate their land and livelihoods and improve agricultural practices for food production security.

Long-term relief actions include the provision of drought-resistant seeds and fertilizers, fishing equipment, livestock and farm tools. With its expertise in farming, livestock, fisheries and forestry, FAO also provides information on rehabilitation, local food security and agricultural needs.

FAO's Special Programme for Food Security (SPFS) targets small-scale farmers by implementing low-cost technologies to increase profits, food and livestock production. The programme introduces improved breeds and high value crops like rice, maze and onions as sources of farmers' income.

FAO also helps rehabilitate dams and introduces low-cost equipment (pedal or motorized pumps) for a consistent supply of water for food production.

World Food Programme (WFP)

The World Food Programme (WFP)'s Protracted Relief and Recovery Operations (PRROs) facilitate the transition from relief to recovery in a wide range of areas, from education to community infrastructure to food assistance.

The School Meals programme promises a nutritious meal—a mid-morning snack or breakfast—to children who attend school. Not only does the scheme provide vital

A WFP food-for-work project provided over half a million people with more than 10,000 tons of food during a single month.

nourishment for hungry children, but it also keeps them at school, where they learn essential skills in a safe environment. WFP's "take-home rations" project is especially designed to encourage education for young girls, by providing a sack of rice and a can of cooking oil to families who send their daughters to school.

WFP also operates cash-for-work and food-for-work programmes in rural areas to help inhabitants generate income by participating in the resilience-building effort.

United Nations Children's Fund (UNICEF)

The United Nations Children's Fund (UNICEF)'s primary goal is to rebuild a protective and healthy environment for children and their families. In response to emergencies that require a long-term relief response, UNICEF covers areas that directly affect the health and well-being of children.

Through UNICEF's Back to School Campaigns, children participate in peacebuilding efforts and demobilization programmes and learn how to support community reconciliation. UNICEF also organizes tracing and family reunification programmes for children who are displaced or orphaned.

A UNICEF staff member demonstrates good hand-washing techniques during the cholera prevention campaign in Port-au-Prince, Haiti.

World Health Organization (WHO)

The World Health Organization (WHO) promotes health and sponsors prevention and education activities for a variety of population groups. The long-term response activities of WHO include reconstructing housing with improved local drainage and built-in roof water-catchment systems, rebuilding markets with adequate hygienic facilities and repairing and deepening rural wells and boreholes.

United Nations High Commissioner for Refugees (UNHCR)

During or after major refugee crises, the Office of the United Nations High Commissioner for Refugees (UNHCR) helps refugees and other forcibly displaced persons rebuild their lives in peace and dignity.

A refugee's voluntary repatriation to her or his country or region of origin is considered the most successful outcome of all. Upon a refugee's return home, UNHCR organizes

FOCUS ON

UNHCR GOODWILL AMBASSADOR ANGELINA JOLIE

Actress Angelina Jolie actively supports the humanitarian work of the United Nations for refugees. Since her appointment as a Goodwill Ambassador in early 2001, she has visited more than 20 countries to highlight dire refugee situations and people's needs for protection and support from the international community.

In March 2011, Jolie visited a warehouse in Kabul, Afghanistan, that is now serving as a home for many Afghan refugees and IDPs. There she again met Khanum Gul and her son, whom Jolie had encountered during her previous visit, in 2008. Like most returnees who came back after years of exile, Khanum and her husband are still living in the trap of hunger and poverty with a lack of basic amenities. They do not have enough food for their family, including their 3-year-old son, who suffers from developmental delays due to malnutrition and lack of medical care.

During her trip, Jolie also met with a 10-year-old girl, Sahira, from the village of Qala Gadu, where nearly all of the 2,500 families are either returned refugees or IDPs. Sahira is the first of five girls in her family to attend school—one of the schools funded by Jolie—and wants to become a doctor when she grows up.

The stories of Khanum's family and Sahira show that returnees need continuous support and attention from the international community, as many of them continue to live without access to jobs, education opportunities and medical services.

"go-and-see" follow-up visits and provides safety information while engaging in community reconciliation activities and providing legal aid.

Refugees who cannot return home often locally integrate into host societies or resettle in a third country. In such cases, UNHCR supports integration programmes, such as cultural orientation, language and vocational training, and offers legal advice as well as psychological support to ensure that people are well integrated.

FOCUS ON

PEOPLE OF CONCERN: FORCIBLY DISPLACED PERSONS

Refugees
» A refugee is someone who fled his or her home and country owing to "a well-founded fear of persecution because of his/her race, religion, nationality, membership in a particular social group, or political opinion", according to the United Nations 1951 Refugee Convention. Many refugees are in exile to escape the effects of natural or human-made disasters. There are 10.4 million refugees of concern to the UNHCR today, more than half in Asia and some 20 per cent in Africa.

Asylum seeker
» Asylum seekers say they are refugees and have fled their homes as refugees do, but their claim to refugee status is not yet definitively evaluated in the country to which they fled. UNHCR's recent reports reveal that a total of 358,800 asylum seekers lodged their asylum applications in 2011. This is nearly half of the 620,000 applications filed a decade ago, in 2001.

Internally displaced persons (IDPs)
» IDPs are people who have not crossed an international border but have moved to a different region than the one they call home within their own country. There are an estimated 15.6 million IDPs under the concern of the UNHCR in 22 countries, including Sudan, Colombia and Iraq, the three countries with the largest IDP populations.

Stateless persons
» Stateless persons do not have a recognized nationality and do not belong to any country. There are approximately 12 million stateless people across Africa, the Americas, Asia and Europe. Statelessness situations are usually caused by discrimination against certain groups. Their lack of identification—a citizenship certificate—can exclude them from access to important government services, including health care, education or employment.

Returnees
» Returnees are former refugees who return to their own countries or regions of origin after time in exile. Returnees need continuous support and reintegration assistance to ensure that they can rebuild their lives at home. In 2009, more than five million IDPs and 251,000 refugees were reported to have returned home.

A woman stands in Zam Zam IDP Camp in El Fasher, North Darfur, established after political clashes between the Government of Sudan and rebel forces.

EMERGENCY PREPAREDNESS AND PREVENTION

Nothing is better than prevention. Although some natural or man-made disasters are difficult to predict, it is possible to reduce the risks from recurring disasters and prepare in advance in regions that are particularly prone to such extreme events. With the right preparedness, many more lives can be saved with much less effort. Before short-term or long-term relief efforts are even needed, United Nations agencies work with governments and other humanitarian organizations to prepare for and build resilience against future crises.

Improving living conditions

One such effort is to break the trap of poverty and hunger. The World Food Programme (WFP) and the United Nations Food and Agriculture Organization (FAO) provide information on world food security problems, including weather conditions for agriculture and crop prospects. FAO's Global Information and Early Warning System (GIEWS) provides early warnings of food crises, and its Emergency Prevention System (EMPRES) helps to protect the entire food chain against the spread of animal and

The United Nations provides assistance in building infrastructure both before and after a crisis. Good infrastructures are key to improving economic situations and crucial for humanitarian aid to reach more people in a shorter period of time.

plant disease. As an effort to increase food security and agriculture in local communities, the FAO assists in the construction of agricultural infrastructure, including roads, warehouses and irrigation. The United Nations Development Programme (UNDP) also participates in the construction of community infrastructure to help prevent future crises, for instance the rehabilitation of watersheds to reduce the risk of floods in regions particularly prone to them.

Reducing the impact of disasters

The United Nations International Strategy for Disaster Reduction (UNISDR) coordinates risk reduction activities and proposes strategic ways to reduce the impact of natural hazards. Its priorities are mainly directed to developing countries, where 85 per cent of the populations are exposed to natural disasters. UNISDR organizes and participates in various disaster risk reduction events around the world. It works with local communities, other international organizations, non-governmental organizations, private enterprises, governments and other stakeholders to raise awareness of dangers, encourage preparedness, and foster resilience in areas that are at risk such as Fiji (floods), Texas, USA (wildfires), and the Philippines (typhoons).

The United Nations Children's Fund (UNICEF) has various ongoing prevention programmes, including an HIV/AIDS campaign, "United for Children, United Against AIDS," that focuses on the prevention of mother-to-child transmission and HIV infection among teenagers and young people. UNICEF provides preventive treatment, reproductive health services, childbirth care and pediatric HIV care, counseling and psychological support for those who are affected, as well as information on HIV prevention and testing for young people in high-risk communities. The World Health Organization (WHO) also works to reduce high-risk factors that lead to health-related emergencies by supporting prevention campaigns and helping communities develop and improve essential health-care plans.

FOCUS ON

HELPING A VILLAGE HELP ITSELF, LINKING RELIEF AND RECOVERY[12]

Thin Thin Aye, 31, used to make a living cutting and selling firewood. But the May 2008 Nargis cyclone in Myanmar wiped away her house, the wood and all her hand tools. Her remaining family survives on rice rations from agencies and NGOs.

The United Nations Development Programme (UNDP) helped the people of the village decide who would receive different types of recovery assistance.

After several hours of animated discussions, the villagers selected 30 families, including Thin Thin Aye's, as the most vulnerable households, making each one eligible for a $40 grant. With the grant, villagers could purchase any materials they needed right away.

The villagers also selected the households in need of shelter assistance. When these households received financial assistance from UNDP, they were able to use the cash to rebuild their houses.

Lastly, another 55 per cent of the households were selected by the villagers to receive cash grants and in-kind assistance to help them resume their livelihoods.

---

[12] United Nations Cyberschoolbus, "The United Nations in our Daily Lives: United Nations Development Programme," *http://cyberschoolbus.un.org/ourlives/undp.asp*

Humanitarian action for economic and social development

Many of the United Nations agencies' preparedness and prevention programmes directly address the United Nations Millennium Development Goals—for instance, to halve hunger and poverty, achieve universal primary education and gender parity in education and combat HIV/AIDS by the end of 2015—all with the ultimate goal of overcoming the world's epidemic emergencies and crises.

FOCUS ON

THE HORN OF AFRICA: MULTIPLE THREATS OF HUNGER AND MALNUTRITION

The people in the Horn of Africa have struggled against food and nutrition crises brought about by a devastating drought for nearly three decades. During 2010-2012, rainfall was recorded at less than 30 per cent of the 1995-2010 average, causing crop failure, delayed harvests and heavy livestock mortality. And just to make things worse, since the outbreak of civil war in Somalia in 1991, there has been no central government control over most of the country's territory. The United Nations has had to base operations to assist the country and its people in neighbouring Kenya.

Malnutrition and mortality rates are alarmingly high in these regions. The estimated number of people needing food and other basic humanitarian services stands at 12.4 million today, including those in Djibouti, Ethiopia, Kenya, Somalia and Uganda.

Somalia is one of the countries worst affected by this severe drought. Famine has been declared in two of the country's southern regions, and one quarter of 7.5 million Somalis are displaced, some fleeing to Ethiopia and Kenya.

The United Nations Food and Agriculture Organization (FAO) has issued agricultural recovery actions across the Horn of Africa to help save more lives and livelihoods in drought-struck regions. Its interventions include distribution of seeds, livestock vaccination and treatment and cash-for-work programmes.

A high-level operational meeting was organized in August 2011 to address the long-term problem of food insecurity and crisis and to identify programmes and projects to build resilience over the short, medium and long terms across the area. Agriculture ministers of all FAO's member countries were invited, along with senior officials from regional economic organizations, the African Union, United Nations agencies, NGOs and other partners.

TEST YOUR KNOWLEDGE

1. What kind of disasters do humanitarian workers respond to?

2. What kind of disaster strikes most often nowadays?

3. Briefly describe two of the latest disasters that have affected people across the globe.

4. True or false: education is a key humanitarian need.

5. Who is involved in providing humanitarian aid?

6. How long does it take for a United Nations Disaster Assessment and Coordination team to arrive at an area affected by a crisis: 3-12 hours, 12-48 hours, or 48-72 hours?

7. What does OCHA stand for?

8. Does OCHA coordinate the activities of all humanitarian workers, regardless of their affiliation with the United Nations?

9. Why is humanitarian response organized in clusters?

10. What agency is in charge of the refugees cluster?

11. Everyone talks about humanitarian workers, but do you know what they actually do?

12. Which Organization fights epidemic outbreaks?

13. What does WFP do for people affected by a crisis? How long does it take them to react?

14. Who is in charge of coordinating assistance to IDPs?

15. What is the difference between a refugee and an asylum seeker?

16. Why are stateless persons marginalized?

17. List the five key activities on which long-term emergency responses focus.

18. Why should special attention be paid to men and boys?

19. Once a refugee, always a refugee? Can refugees go back home, and if so, what does the United Nations do to help them?

20. Can disaster reoccurrences be prevented?

CHAPTER 7

ADDITIONAL
INFORMATION

FREQUENTLY ASKED QUESTIONS

CAN INDIVIDUALS JOIN THE UNITED NATIONS AS MEMBERS?

No, only independent countries with international recognition from other States can become members of the United Nations.

HOW CAN INDIVIDUALS SUPPORT THE UNITED NATIONS?

Individuals can support the work of the United Nations through international and local non-governmental organizations (NGOs). Some of them collaborate with the United Nations Department of Public Information and provide the United Nations with valuable links to people around the world.

United Nations Associations

There are United Nations Associations in more than 100 countries, often with many local chapters (e.g. UNA-Australia, UNA-Canada, UNA-New Zealand, UNA-South Africa, UNA-UK, etc.), as well as the global union of national associations, the World Federation of United Nations Associations (WFUNA).

Most United Nations Associations have youth programmes and wings either within their scope of work or as separate United Nations Youth Associations (UNYA). You can find out more about how youth can get involved by contacting your local UNA directly.

For more information, visit the site of the World Federation of United Nations Association: *http://www.wfuna.org/.*

National offices of United Nations agencies

The United Nations Children's Fund (UNICEF) has national committees in many countries that spread awareness about UNICEF's programmes and raise funds to help them become a reality.

Some 3,600 United Nations Educational, Scientific and Cultural Organization (UNESCO) clubs, centres and associations (all affiliated with UNESCO) in over 90 countries undertake activities in the areas of education, science, culture and communication.

United Nations Information Centres (UNICs)

The United Nations maintains Information Centres (UNICs) and other major contact points all over the world.

You can find a list of UNICs on page 214 and online: *http://unic.un.org*

United Nations Volunteers (UNV)

If you have a skill in such fields as agriculture, medicine, education, information technology, vocational training, the promotion of human rights or industry—as well as the necessary flexibility and commitment—the United Nations Volunteers (UNV) programme may be right for you. The programme places volunteers, for a one-to-two-year period, with an appropriate United Nations development project in a developing country.

For more information on the programme, visit *http://www.unv.org*

Campaigns and social media

You can get involved in specific campaigns advertized throughout the United Nations and those of other organizations in the United Nations family. These campaigns aim to feed hungry people, stop rape in conflict, eliminate violence against women, end child labour and more. Online resources for many of the campaigns are listed at the end of this chapter.

You can also participate in the conversation on social media such as Facebook and Twitter. The UN family has a significant presence in social media, one example being *http://www.facebook.com/unpublications*

HOW CAN YOUNG PEOPLE GET TO KNOW AND EXPERIENCE THE UNITED NATIONS?

Young people are a top priority for the United Nations, as they represent a new generation of support. Several hundred Model United Nations conferences are organized every year at all educational levels, from primary school to university, in many different configurations and countries. Many of today's leaders in law, government, business and the arts participated in Model United Nations programmes during their youth.

At the Global Model United Nations (GMUN) Conference, students from every region of the world role-play as foreign diplomats and participate in simulated sessions of the United Nations General Assembly and other multilateral bodies in the United Nations system. While preparing for a Model United Nations conference, students develop leadership, research, writing, public speaking and problem-solving skills that they will use throughout their lives. In addition, participation encourages consensus building, conflict resolution and cooperation.

Global Model United Nations offers two unique innovations:

> » It uses Rules of Procedure that more closely represent how the United Nations functions.

> » It provides unparalleled access to United Nations officials and diplomats prior to and during the conference.

Each delegation representing a Member State is made up of students from different countries.

I want to continue my studies at a foreign university. Can the United Nations provide me with financial assistance?

The United Nations does not provide financial assistance to students and has no general scholarship or student exchange programme.

Does the United Nations accept student interns?

The United Nations provides opportunities for students enrolled in a graduate programme to undertake an internship at its Headquarters in New York and at other major locations of the Organization.

You can find more information on the internship programme at *http://www.un.org/depts/ OHRM/sds/internsh/index.htm* or *http://social.un.org/index/Youth/UNOpportunities/ Internships.aspx.*

I want to work at the United Nations. What should I do?

The United Nations Secretariat is looking for competent and motivated individuals with a strong belief in the Organization's purpose and mandates, who are willing to dedicate themselves to a rewarding international career in different locations around the world. The United Nations provides an opportunity to serve in a dynamic, multicultural environment in a variety of jobs in the support of global causes.

If you are exploring the possibility of a career with the United Nations, browse the job openings and apply. All job openings in the United Nations Secretariat are published on the United Nations Careers Portal, careers.un.org (also available in French). There, you can create your profile, review available listings and submit your application online.

Candidates for jobs in the General Service and related categories, including those in the trades and crafts, security and safety, secretarial and other support positions, are recruited locally.

Competitive examinations

The United Nations offers the Young Professionals Programme for Junior Professionals, a recruitment initiative that brings new talent to the Organization through an annual entrance examination. The United Nations also holds examinations for positions requiring special language skills. Information on both types of competitive examinations is available online at *careers.un.org*

Associate Experts Programme

This programme offers young professionals who are graduates from universities or institutions of higher education an opportunity to work on development or regional projects and acquire professional experience in their fields with the technical cooperation of the United Nations Secretariat.

More information on the programme can be found at *http://esa.un.org/techcoop/associateexperts/index.html*

Job opportunities in the United Nations System

If you are interested in working for other United Nations agencies, funds or programmes, please visit their websites directly. Most websites can be accessed through the links found at the International Civil Service Commission: *http://icsc.un.org/secretariat/includes/joblinks.asp*

Warning to applicants

There are job advertisements and offers that falsely state that they are from the United Nations. Please be aware that the United Nations does not request payment at any stage of the application and review process.

Where can I get information about a United Nations Member country's position on various current issues?

You can obtain such information from the Permanent Mission to the United Nations of the country concerned. The list of contact information and websites for the Member States can be found at *http://www.un.org/en/members*

UNITED NATIONS OBSERVANCES

United Nations observances contribute to the achievement of the purposes of the UN Charter and promote awareness of and action on important political, social, cultural, humanitarian or human rights issues. They provide a useful means for the promotion of international and national action and stimulate interest in United Nations activities and programmes.

For more information, visit *un.org/en/events/observances/index.shtml*

DECADES

2011-2020	Third International Decade for the Eradication of Colonialism
	United Nations Decade on Biodiversity
	Decade of Action for Road Safety
2010-2020	United Nations Decade for Deserts and the Fight against Desertification
2008-2017	Second United Nations Decade for the Eradication of Poverty
2006-2016	Decade of Recovery and Sustainable Development of the Affected Regions (third decade after the Chernobyl disaster)
2005-2015	International Decade for Action: Water for Life
2005-2014	United Nations Decade of Education for Sustainable Development
	Second International Decade of the World's Indigenous People
2003-2012	United Nations Literacy Decade: Education for All

YEARS

2014	International Year of Family Farming
2013	International Year of Water Cooperation
	International Year of Quinoa
2012	International Year of Cooperatives
	International Year of Sustainable Energy for All

DAYS AND WEEKS

January	27	International Day of Commemoration in Memory of the Victims of the Holocaust
February	1st week	World Interfaith Harmony Week
	4	World Cancer Day
	6	International Day of Zero Tolerance to Female Genital Mutilation [WHO]
	13	World Radio Day
	20	World Day of Social Justice
	21	International Mother Language Day [UNESCO]
March	8	International Women's Day
	21	International Day for the Elimination of Racial Discrimination
	21	World Down Syndrome Day
	21	World Poetry Day [UNESCO]
	21	International Day of Nowruz
	21-27	Week of Solidarity with the Peoples Struggling against Racism and Racial Discrimination
	22	World Water Day
	23	World Meteorological Day [WMO]
	24	World Tuberculosis Day [WHO]
	24	International Day for the Right to the Truth Concerning Gross Human Rights Violations and for the Dignity of Victims
	25	International Day of Remembrance of the Victims of Slavery and the Transatlantic Slave Trade
	25	International Day of Solidarity with Detained and Missing Staff Members
April	2	World Autism Awareness Day
	4	International Day for Mine Awareness and Assistance in Mine Action
	7	Day of Remembrance of the Victims of the Rwanda Genocide
	7	World Health Day [WHO]
	12	International Day of Human Space Flight
	22	International Mother Earth Day
	23	World Book and Copyright Day [UNESCO]

April (continued)	25	World Malaria Day [WHO]
	26	World Intellectual Property Day [WIPO]
	28	World Day for Safety and Health at Work [ILO]
	29	Day of Remembrance for all Victims of Chemical Warfare
	29	International Jazz Day [UNESCO]
May	Full Moon	Day of Vesak
	3	World Press Freedom Day
	8–9	Time of Remembrance and Reconciliation for Those Who Lost Their Lives during the Second World War
	14–15	World Migratory Bird Day [UNEP]
	15	International Day of Families
	17	World Telecommunication and Information Society Day [ITU]
	21	World Day for Cultural Diversity for Dialogue and Development
	22	International Day for Biological Diversity
	25-31	Week of Solidarity with the Peoples of Non-Self-Governing Territories
	29	International Day of United Nations Peacekeepers
	31	World No-Tobacco Day [WHO]
June	4	International Day of Innocent Children Victims of Aggression
	5	World Environment Day [UNEP]
	8	World Oceans Day
	12	World Day Against Child Labour [ILO]
	14	World Blood Donor Day [WHO]
	17	World Day to Combat Desertification and Drought
	20	World Refugee Day
	23	United Nations Public Service Day
	23	International Widow's Day
	25	Day of the Seafarer [IMO]
	26	International Day against Drug Abuse and Illicit Trafficking
	26	United Nations International Day in Support of Victims of Torture

July	1st Saturday	International Day of Cooperatives
	11	World Population Day
	18	Nelson Mandela International Day
	28	World Hepatitis Day [WHO]
	30	International Day of Friendship
August	1–7	World Breastfeeding Week [WHO]
	9	International Day of the World's Indigenous People
	12	International Youth Day
	19	World Humanitarian Day
	23	International Day for the Remembrance of the Slave Trade and its Abolition [UNESCO]
	29	International Day against Nuclear Tests
	30	International Day of the Victims of Enforced Disappearances
September	8	International Literacy Day [UNESCO]
	10	World Suicide Prevention Day [WHO]
	15	International Day of Democracy
	16	International Day for the Preservation of the Ozone Layer
	21	International Day of Peace
	Last Sunday	World Heart Day [WHO]
	27	World Tourism Day [UNWTO]
	28	World Rabies Day [WHO]
	Last week	World Maritime Day [IMO]
October	1	International Day of Older Persons
	2	International Day of Non-Violence
	1st Monday	World Habitat Day
	4-10	World Space Week
	5	World Teachers' Day [UNESCO]
	9	World Post Day [UPU]
	10	World Mental Health Day [WHO]
	2nd Thursday	World Sight Day [WHO]
	11	International Day of the Girl Child
	13	International Day for Disaster Reduction
	15	International Day of Rural Women

October *(continued)*	16	World Food Day [FAO]
	17	International Day for the Eradication of Poverty
	20	World Statistics Day
	24	United Nations Day
	24	World Development Information Day
	24-30	Disarmament Week
	27	World Day for Audiovisual Heritage [UNESCO]
November	6	International Day for Preventing the Exploitation of the Environment in War and Armed Conflict
	10	World Science Day for Peace and Development [UNESCO]
	Week of 11	International Week of Science and Peace
	12	World Pneumonia Day [WHO]
	14	World Diabetes Day [WHO]
	16	International Day for Tolerance
	3rd Thursday	World Philosophy Day [UNESCO]
	17	World Chronic Obstructive Pulmonary Disease Day [WHO]
	20	Universal Children's Day
	20	Africa Industrialization Day
	3rd Sunday	World Day of Remembrance for Road Traffic Victims [WHO]
	21	World Television Day
	25	International Day for the Elimination of Violence against Women
	29	International Day of Solidarity with the Palestinian People
December	1	World AIDS Day
	2	International Day for the Abolition of Slavery
	3	International Day of Persons with Disabilities
	5	International Volunteer Day for Economic and Social Development
	7	International Civil Aviation Day [ICAO]
	9	International Anti-Corruption Day
	10	Human Rights Day
	11	International Mountain Day
	18	International Migrants Day
	19	United Nations Day for South-South Cooperation
	20	International Human Solidarity Day

THE UNITED NATIONS SYSTEM

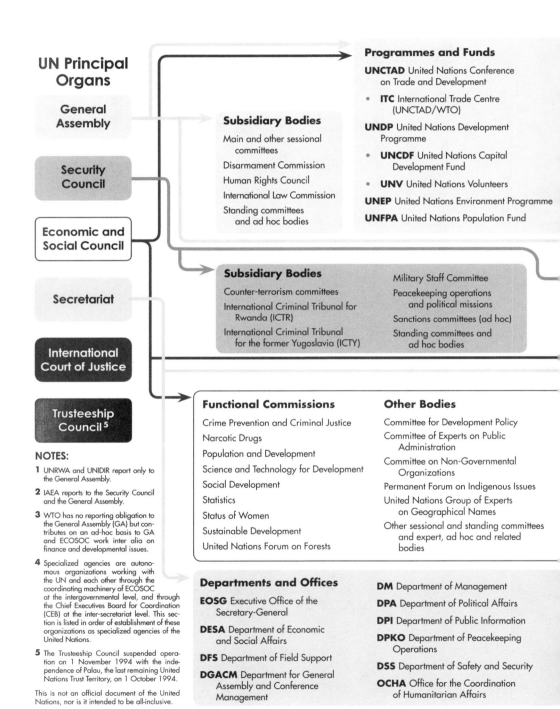

UN Principal Organs

- General Assembly
- Security Council
- Economic and Social Council
- Secretariat
- International Court of Justice
- Trusteeship Council [5]

Programmes and Funds

UNCTAD United Nations Conference on Trade and Development

- **ITC** International Trade Centre (UNCTAD/WTO)

UNDP United Nations Development Programme

- **UNCDF** United Nations Capital Development Fund
- **UNV** United Nations Volunteers

UNEP United Nations Environment Programme

UNFPA United Nations Population Fund

Subsidiary Bodies

Main and other sessional committees

Disarmament Commission

Human Rights Council

International Law Commission

Standing committees and ad hoc bodies

Subsidiary Bodies

Counter-terrorism committees

International Criminal Tribunal for Rwanda (ICTR)

International Criminal Tribunal for the former Yugoslavia (ICTY)

Military Staff Committee

Peacekeeping operations and political missions

Sanctions committees (ad hoc)

Standing committees and ad hoc bodies

Functional Commissions

Crime Prevention and Criminal Justice

Narcotic Drugs

Population and Development

Science and Technology for Development

Social Development

Statistics

Status of Women

Sustainable Development

United Nations Forum on Forests

Other Bodies

Committee for Development Policy

Committee of Experts on Public Administration

Committee on Non-Governmental Organizations

Permanent Forum on Indigenous Issues

United Nations Group of Experts on Geographical Names

Other sessional and standing committees and expert, ad hoc and related bodies

Departments and Offices

EOSG Executive Office of the Secretary-General

DESA Department of Economic and Social Affairs

DFS Department of Field Support

DGACM Department for General Assembly and Conference Management

DM Department of Management

DPA Department of Political Affairs

DPI Department of Public Information

DPKO Department of Peacekeeping Operations

DSS Department of Safety and Security

OCHA Office for the Coordination of Humanitarian Affairs

NOTES:

1 UNRWA and UNIDIR report only to the General Assembly.

2 IAEA reports to the Security Council and the General Assembly.

3 WTO has no reporting obligation to the General Assembly (GA) but contributes on an ad-hoc basis to GA and ECOSOC work inter alia on finance and developmental issues.

4 Specialized agencies are autonomous organizations working with the UN and each other through the coordinating machinery of ECOSOC at the intergovernmental level, and through the Chief Executives Board for Coordination (CEB) at the inter-secretariat level. This section is listed in order of establishment of these organizations as specialized agencies of the United Nations.

5 The Trusteeship Council suspended operation on 1 November 1994 with the independence of Palau, the last remaining United Nations Trust Territory, on 1 October 1994.

This is not an official document of the United Nations, nor is it intended to be all-inclusive.

UN-HABITAT United Nations Human Settlements Programme

UNHCR Office of the United Nations High Commissioner for Refugees

UNICEF United Nations Children's Fund

UNODC United Nations Office on Drugs and Crime

UNRWA[1] United Nations Relief and Works Agency for Palestine Refugees in the Near East

UN-Women United Nations Entity for Gender Equality and the Empowerment of Women

WFP World Food Programme

Research and Training Institutes

UNICRI United Nations Interregional Crime and Justice Research Institute

UNIDIR[1] United Nations Institute for Disarmament Research

UNITAR United Nations Institute for Training and Research

UNRISD United Nations Research Institute for Social Development

UNSSC United Nations System Staff College

UNU United Nations University

Other Entities

UNAIDS Joint United Nations Programme on HIV/AIDS

UNISDR United Nations International Strategy for Disaster Reduction

UNOPS United Nations Office for Project Services

Related Organizations

CTBTO PrepCom Preparatory Commission for the Comprehensive Nuclear-Test-Ban Treaty Organization

IAEA[2] International Atomic Energy Agency

OPCW Organisation for the Prohibition of Chemical Weapons

WTO[3] World Trade Organization

Advisory Subsidiary Body

UN Peacebuilding Commission

Specialized Agencies[4]

ILO International Labour Organization

FAO Food and Agriculture Organization of the United Nations

UNESCO United Nations Educational, Scientific and Cultural Organization

WHO World Health Organization

World Bank Group

- **IBRD** International Bank for Reconstruction and Development
- **IDA** International Development Association
- **IFC** International Finance Corporation
- **MIGA** Multilateral Investment Guarantee Agency
- **ICSID** International Centre for Settlement of Investment Disputes

IMF International Monetary Fund

ICAO International Civil Aviation Organization

IMO International Maritime Organization

ITU International Telecommunication Union

UPU Universal Postal Union

WMO World Meteorological Organization

WIPO World Intellectual Property Organization

IFAD International Fund for Agricultural Development

UNIDO United Nations Industrial Development Organization

UNWTO World Tourism Organization

Regional Commissions

ECA Economic Commission for Africa

ECE Economic Commission for Europe

ECLAC Economic Commission for Latin America and the Caribbean

ESCAP Economic and Social Commission for Asia and the Pacific

ESCWA Economic and Social Commission for Western Asia

OHCHR Office of the United Nations High Commissioner for Human Rights

OIOS Office of Internal Oversight Services

OLA Office of Legal Affairs

OSAA Office of the Special Adviser on Africa

OSRSG/CAAC Office of the Special Representative of the Secretary-General for Children and Armed Conflict

UNODA Office for Disarmament Affairs

UNOG United Nations Office at Geneva

UN-OHRLLS Office of the High Representative for the Least Developed Countries, Landlocked Developing Countries and Small Island Developing States

UNON United Nations Office at Nairobi

UNOV United Nations Office at Vienna

2011 Rev.2

MEMBER STATES

Membership in the United Nations has grown from 51 States in 1945 to 193 in 2012. States are admitted by decision of the General Assembly upon recommendation of the Security Council.

MEMBER STATE	POPULATION (EST.) FOR 2010	DATE OF ADMISSION
Afghanistan	29,117,000	19 November 1946
Albania	3,169,000	14 December 1955
Algeria	35,423,000	8 October 1962
Andorra	87,000	28 July 1993
Angola	18,993,000	1 December 1976
Antigua and Barbuda	89,000	11 November 1981
Argentina	40,666,000	24 October 1945
Armenia	3,090,000	2 March 1992
Australia	21,512,000	1 November 1945
Austria	8,387,000	14 December 1955
Azerbaijan	8,934,000	2 March 1992
Bahamas	346,000	18 September 1973
Bahrain	807,000	21 September 1971
Bangladesh	164,425,000	17 September 1974
Barbados	257,000	9 December 1966
Belarus	9,588,000	24 October 1945
Belgium	10,698,000	27 December 1945
Belize	313,000	25 September 1981
Benin	9,212,000	20 September 1960
Bhutan	708,000	21 September 1971
Bolivia (Plurinational State of)	10,031,000	14 November 1945
Bosnia and Herzegovina	3,760,000	22 May 1992
Botswana	1,978,000	17 October 1966
Brazil	195,423,000	24 October 1945
Brunei Darussalam	407,000	21 September 1984
Bulgaria	7,497,000	14 December 1955

Burkina Faso	16,287,000	20 September 1960
Burundi	8,519,000	18 September 1962
Cambodia	15,053,000	14 December 1955
Cameroon	19,958,000	20 September 1960
Canada	33,890,000	9 November 1945
Cape Verde	513,000	16 September 1975
Central African Republic	4,506,000	20 September 1960
Chad	11,506,000	20 September 1960
Chile	17,135,000	24 October 1945
China	1,354,146,000	24 October 1945
Colombia	46,300,000	5 November 1945
Comoros	691,000	12 November 1975
Congo	3,759,000	20 September 1960
Costa Rica	4,640,000	2 November 1945
Côte d'Ivoire	21,571,000	20 September 1960
Croatia	4,410,000	22 May 1992
Cuba	11,204,000	24 October 1945
Cyprus	880,000	20 September 1960
Czech Republic	10,411,000	19 January 1993
Democratic People's Republic of Korea	23,991,000	17 September 1991
Democratic Republic of the Congo	67,827,000	20 September 1960
Denmark	5,481,000	24 October 1945
Djibouti	879,000	20 September 1977
Dominica	67,000	18 December 1978
Dominican Republic	10,225,000	24 October 1945
Ecuador	13,775,000	21 December 1945
Egypt	84,474,000	24 October 1945
El Salvador	6,194,000	24 October 1945
Equatorial Guinea	693,000	12 November 1968
Eritrea	5,224,000	28 May 1993
Estonia	1,339,000	17 September 1991
Ethiopia	84,976,000	13 November 1945
Fiji	854,000	13 October 1970
Finland	5,346,000	14 December 1955

France	62,637,000	24 October 1945
Gabon	1,501,000	20 September 1960
Gambia	1,751,000	21 September 1965
Georgia	4,219,000	31 July 1992
Germany	82,057,000	18 September 1973
Ghana	24,333,000	8 March 1957
Greece	11,183,000	25 October 1945
Grenada	104,000	17 September 1974
Guatemala	14,377,000	21 November 1945
Guinea	10,324,000	12 December 1958
Guinea-Bissau	1,647,000	17 September 1974
Guyana	761,000	20 September 1966
Haiti	10,188,000	24 October 1945
Honduras	7,616,000	17 December 1945
Hungary	9,973,000	14 December 1955
Iceland	329,000	19 November 1946
India	1,214,464,000	30 October 1945
Indonesia	232,517,000	28 September 1950
Iran (Islamic Republic of)	75,078,000	24 October 1945
Iraq	31,467,000	21 December 1945
Ireland	4,589,000	14 December 1955
Israel	7,285,000	11 May 1949
Italy	60,098,000	14 December 1955
Jamaica	2,730,000	18 September 1962
Japan	126,995,000	18 December 1956
Jordan	6,472,000	14 December 1955
Kazakhstan	15,753,000	2 March 1992
Kenya	40,863,000	16 December 1963
Kiribati	100,000	14 September 1999
Kuwait	3,051,000	14 May 1963
Kyrgyzstan	5,550,000	2 March 1992
Lao People's Democratic Republic	6,436,000	14 December 1955
Latvia	2,240,000	17 September 1991
Lebanon	4,255,000	24 October 1945

Lesotho	2,084,000	17 October 1966
Liberia	4,102,000	2 November 1945
Libya	6,546,000	14 December 1955
Liechtenstein	36,000	18 September 1990
Lithuania	3,255,000	17 September 1991
Luxembourg	492,000	24 October 1945
Madagascar	20,146,000	20 September 1960
Malawi	15,692,000	1 December 1964
Malaysia	27,914,000	17 September 1957
Maldives	314,000	21 September 1965
Mali	13,323,000	28 September 1960
Malta	410,000	1 December 1964
Marshall Islands	63,000	17 September 1991
Mauritania	3,366,000	27 October 1961
Mauritius	1,297,000	24 April 1968
Mexico	110,645,000	7 November 1945
Micronesia (Federated States of)	111,000	17 September 1991
Moldova (Republic of)	3,576,000	2 March 1992
Monaco	33,000	28 May 1993
Mongolia	2,701,000	27 October 1961
Montenegro	626,000	28 June 2006
Morocco	32,381,000	12 November 1956
Mozambique	23,406,000	16 September 1975
Myanmar	50,496,000	19 April 1948
Namibia	2,212,000	23 April 1990
Nauru	10,000	14 September 1999
Nepal	29,853,000	14 December 1955
Netherlands	16,653,000	10 December 1945
New Zealand	4,303,000	24 October 1945
Nicaragua	5,822,000	24 October 1945
Niger	15,891,000	20 September 1960
Nigeria	158,259,000	7 October 1960
Norway	4,855,000	27 November 1945
Oman	2,905,000	7 October 1971

Pakistan	184,753,000	30 September 1947
Palau	21,000	15 December 1994
Panama	3,508,000	13 November 1945
Papua New Guinea	6,888,000	10 October 1975
Paraguay	6,460,000	24 October 1945
Peru	29,496,000	31 October 1945
Philippines	93,617,000	24 October 1945
Poland	38,038,000	24 October 1945
Portugal	10,732,000	14 December 1955
Qatar	1,508,000	21 September 1971
Republic of Korea	48,501,000	17 September 1991
Romania	21,190,000	14 December 1955
Russian Federation	140,367,000	24 October 1945
Rwanda	10,277,000	18 September 1962
Saint Kitts and Nevis	52,000	23 September 1983
Saint Lucia	174,000	18 September 1979
Saint Vincent and the Grenadines	109,000	16 September 1980
Samoa	179,000	15 December 1976
San Marino	32,000	2 March 1992
Sao Tome and Principe	165,000	16 September 1975
Saudi Arabia	26,246,000	24 October 1945
Senegal	12,861,000	28 September 1960
Serbia	9,856,000	1 November 2000
Seychelles	85,000	21 September 1976
Sierra Leone	5,836,000	27 September 1961
Singapore	4,837,000	21 September 1965
Slovakia	5,412,000	19 January 1993
Slovenia	2,025,000	22 May 1992
Solomon Islands	536,000	19 September 1978
Somalia	9,359,000	20 September 1960
South Africa	50,492,000	7 November 1945
South Sudan	8,260,490	14 July 2011
Spain	45,317,000	14 December 1955
Sri Lanka	20,410,000	14 December 1955

Sudan	43,192,000	12 November 1956
Suriname	524,000	4 December 1975
Swaziland	1,202,000	24 September 1968
Sweden	9,293,000	19 November 1946
Switzerland	7,595,000	10 September 2002
Syrian Arab Republic	22,505,000	24 October 1945
Tajikistan	7,075,000	2 March 1992
Thailand	68,139,000	16 December 1946
The former Yugoslav Republic of Macedonia	2,043,000	8 April 1993
Timor-Leste	1,171,000	27 September 2002
Togo	6,780,000	20 September 1960
Tonga	104,000	14 September 1999
Trinidad and Tobago	1,344,000	18 September 1962
Tunisia	10,374,000	12 November 1956
Turkey	75,705,000	24 October 1945
Turkmenistan	5,177,000	2 March 1992
Tuvalu	10,000	5 September 2000
Uganda	33,796,000	25 October 1962
Ukraine	45,433,000	24 October 1945
United Arab Emirates	4,707,000	9 December 1971
United Kingdom	61,899,000	24 October 1945
United Republic of Tanzania	45,040,000	14 December 1961
United States of America	317,641,000	24 October 1945
Uruguay	3,372,000	18 December 1945
Uzbekistan	27,794,000	2 March 1992
Vanuatu	246,000	15 September 1981
Venezuela (Bolivarian Republic of)	29,044,000	15 November 1945
Viet Nam	89,029,000	20 September 1977
Yemen	24,256,000	30 September 1947
Zambia	13,257,000	1 December 1964
Zimbabwe	12,644,000	25 August 1980

REFERENCES AND RESOURCES

PUBLICATIONS

Publications about the United Nations and its activities can be purchased online at the United Nations Publications website, *un.org/publications*. The following are just a few suggested titles:

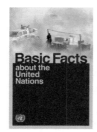

Basic Facts about the United Nations

This comprehensive handbook designed for the general public sets forth the structure of the United Nations, how the Organization works, the main issues it deals with and their importance for people everywhere. Along with explaining the roles played by the UN principal organs and the family of UN organizations, individual chapters explore UN contributions to international peace and security, economic and social development, human rights, humanitarian action, international law and decolonization. A series of appendices documents UN membership, peacekeeping operations, budget and contact information for UN information centers, services and offices. The latest edition of the book has been substantially revised to account for many of the significant developments that have taken place in the world and in the United Nations itself since the last edition (previously titled *The UN Today*), in 2008.

United Nations Charter

Signed on 26 June 1945, the Charter of the United Nations is the Organization's constitutive instrument, setting out the rights and obligations of Member States and establishing the United Nations principal organs and procedures. An international treaty, the Charter codifies basic tenets of international relations, from the sovereign equality of states to the prohibition of the use of force in any manner inconsistent with the purposes of the United Nations. The UN officially came into existence on 24 October 1945 with the ratification of the Charter by its first signatories. Since then, it has continued to grow while remaining true to this pledge—one all the more relevant in the face of the tremendous global transformations that, in the twenty-first century, are confronting humankind.

Universal Declaration of Human Rights

The Universal Declaration of Human Rights is the first international agreement setting out freedoms, rights and entitlements for all of humanity to claim. It emphasizes the inextricable relationship between fundamental freedoms and social justice, and their connection with peace and security. A special edition of the Declaration, beautifully illustrated by French artist Éric Puybaret and designed for a younger audience (primary-school level), is also available.

Yearbook of the United Nations 2008

With its comprehensive coverage of political and security matters, human rights issues, economic and social questions, legal issues, and institutional, administrative and budgetary matters, this Yearbook is the most authoritative reference work available on the activities and concerns of the Organization. Fully indexed, the Yearbook includes the texts of all major General Assembly, Security Council and Economic and Social Council resolutions and decisions. This latest volume, the sixty-second, highlights the conflicts in the Democratic Republic of the Congo, the Georgian province of Abkhazia, and the Sudan, along with the challenges posed by the global food security crisis, severe economic recession, climate change, natural disasters, piracy and terrorism.

The Security Council: Working Methods Handbook

This handbook is designed both for insiders as well as the public at large. It contains an introduction which places the Security Council in the larger context of the United Nations and how it operates. It is followed by practical information on the Security Council agenda, briefings, meetings, programme of work, membership, etc., as well as by the articles of the United Nations Charter related to the work of the Security Council, its Provisional Rules of Procedure, and other documents. It also includes a glossary of terms related to the Security Council.

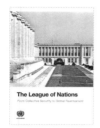

The League of Nations:
From Collective Security to Global Rearmament

In the wake of the First World War, at the Peace Conference at Versailles, US President Wilson called for the creation of a League of Nations for the purpose of affording mutual guarantees of political independence and territorial integrity to great and small nations alike. For the first time, conflicts between nations were a matter of global concern. Numerous key areas — social, economic and statistics, health, labour — were dealt with either directly by the League or indirectly by its specialized agencies. The League, the predecessor to the Untied Nations saw the creation of bodies that would be at the origin of the International Labour Organization, the United Nations Educational, Scientific and Cultural Organization, the World Health Organization and the Office of the United Nations High Commissioner for Refugees.

Dag Hammarskjöld: Instrument, Catalyst, Inspirer

This book compiles selected speeches by former United Nations Secretary-General Dag Hammarskjöld that focus on the role of the United Nations, the role of the Secretary-General in the Organization and the nature of the international civil servant. It is issued in commemoration of the 50 years since the tragic death in a plane crash of Secretary-General Dag Hammarskjöld in September 1961.

The United Nations Disarmament Yearbook

This publication has been a rich source of historical knowledge on developments, trends and achievements of multilateral disarmament for more than 30 years. In early spring of each year, Part I of the Yearbook is published containing an annual compilation of text and statistics on disarmament-related resolutions and decisions of the General Assembly. In early autumn, Part II is published presenting the main topics of multilateral consideration during the year, along with a convenient issues-oriented timeline.

WEBSITES

UNITED NATIONS

United Nations	un.org/en
About the United Nations	un.org/en/aboutun
News and Multimedia	unmultimedia.org
United Nations Visitors Centre	visit.un.org
Publications	un.org/publications
Apps and eBooks	un.org/digital

UN SYSTEM

CTBTO	Preparatory Commission for the Comprehensive Nuclear-Test-Ban Treaty Organization	ctbto.org
FAO	Food and Agriculture Organization	fao.org
IAEA	International Atomic Energy Agency	iaea.org
ICAO	International Civil Aviation Organization	icao.int
IFAD	International Fund for Agricultural Development	ifad.org
ILO	International Labour Organization	ilo.org
IMF	International Monetary Fund	imf.org
IMO	International Maritime Organization	imo.org
ITU	International Telecommunications Union	itu.int
OPCW	Organization for the Prohibition of Chemical Weapons	opcw.org
UNAIDS	Joint United Nations Programme on HIV/AIDS	unaids.org
UNICEF	United Nations Children's Fund	unicef.org
UNCTAD	United Nations Conference on Trade and Development	unctad.org
UNDP	United Nations Development Programme	undp.org
UNEP	United Nations Environment Programme	unep.org
UNESCO	United Nations Educational, Scientific and Cultural Organization	unesco.org
UNFPA	United Nations Population Fund	unfpa.org

UN-Habitat	United Nations Human Settlements Programme	unhabitat.org
UNHCR	United Nations High Commissioner for Refugees	unhcr.org
UNICRI	United Nations Interregional Crime and Justice Research Institute	unicri.it
UNIDIR	United Nations Institute for Disarmament Research	unidir.org
UNIDO	United Nations Industrial Development Organization	unido.org
UNISDR	United Nations International Strategy for Disaster Reduction	unisdr.org
UNITAR	United Nations Institute for Training and Research	unitar.org
UNODC	United Nations Office on Drugs and Crime	unodc.org
UNOPS	United Nations Office for Project Services	unops.org
UNRISD	United Nations Research Institute for Social Development	unrisd.org
UNRWA	United Nations Relief and Works Agency for Palestine Refugees in the Near East	unrwa.org
UNSSC	United Nations System Staff College	unssc.org
UNU	United Nations University	unu.edu
UPU	Universal Postal Union	upu.int
UN-Women	United Nations Entity for Gender Equality and the Empowerment of Women	unwomen.org
UNWTO	World Tourism Organization	unwto.org
World Bank	International Bank for Reconstruction and Development/ The World Bank	worldbank.org
WFP	World Food Programme	wfp.org
WHO	World Health Organization	who.int
WIPO	World Intellectual Property Organization	wipo.int
WMO	World Meteorological Organization	wmo.int
WTO	World Trade Organization	wto.org

FOR YOUNGER AUDIENCES

United Nations Cyberschoolbus	un.org/Pubs/CyberSchoolBus
World Bank – Youthink!	youthink.worldbank.org
WFP – FreeRice	freerice.com
WFP – Food Force	apps.facebook.com/foodforce
UNICEF – Adolescents and youth	unicef.org/adolescence
UNEP – Tunza	unep.org/tunza

GET INVOLVED

Global Model UN	un.org/gmun
UNICEF — Voices of Youth	voicesofyouth.org
UN Volunteers	unv.org
UNODC — Blue Heart Campaign against Human Trafficking	unodc.org/blueheart
UNiTE to End Violence against Women	endviolence.un.org
Stop Rape Now	stoprapenow.org
16 Days of Activism against Gender Violence	unwomen.org/infocus/16-days-of-activism-against-gender-violence
Global Alliance for Cultural Diversity	unesco.org/new/en/culture/themes/cultural-diversity/diversity-of-cultural-expressions/programmes/global-alliance-for-cultural-diversity
SCREAM: Supporting Children's Rights through Education, the Arts and the Media	ilo.org/ipec/Campaignandadvocacy/Scream
United Nations Girls' Education Initiative (UNGEI)	ungei.org
WFP — WeFeedback	wefeedback.org
WFP — Billion for a Billion	wfp.org/donate/1billion
UNICEF — Unite for Children	supportunicef.org
WFP — Students: Get Involved	wfp.org/students-and-teachers/students
United Nations Foundation	unfoundation.org
7 Billion Actions	7billionactions.org
Stand Up against Poverty	standagainstpoverty.org
End Poverty by 2015	endpoverty2015.org
United Nations Citizen Ambassadors	un.org/wcm/content/site/citizenambassadors
FAO — Ending Hunger	endinghunger.org
UNDP — You can make a difference	beta.undp.org/content/undp/en/home/ourwork/get_involved.html
1Goal: Education for All	join1goal.org

UN INFORMATION CENTRES

The network of 63 United Nations Information Centres are key to the Organization's ability to reach the peoples of the world and to share the United Nations story with them in their own languages. These centres, working in coordination with the UN system, reach out to the media and educational institutions, engage in partnerships with governments, local civil society organizations and the private sector, and maintain libraries and electronic information resources.

United Nations Information Centres (UNICs) are the principal sources of information about the United Nations system in the countries where they are located. UNICs are responsible for promoting greater public understanding of and support for the aims and activities of the United Nations by disseminating information on the work of the Organization to people everywhere, especially in developing countries.

By translating information materials into local languages and organizing events to highlight issues or observances, the network of UNICs is one of the main vehicles through which the United Nations reaches out to the world. They give global messages a local accent and help bring the UN closer to the people it serves.

Here is a list of Information Centres per region:

AFRICA			
COUNTRY	UNIC NAME	WEBSITE	EMAIL
Burkina Faso	UNIC Ouagadougou	http://ouagadougou.unic.org	unic.ouagadougou@unic.org
Burundi	UNIC Bujumbura	http://bujumbura.unic.org	unic.bujumbura@unic.org
Cameroon	UNIC Yaounde	http://yaounde.unic.org	unic.yaounde@unic.org
Eritrea	UNO Asmara	http://asmara.unic.org	dpi.er@undp.org
Ghana	UNIC Accra	http://accra.unic.org	unic.accra@unic.org
Kenya	UNIC Nairobi	http://www.unicnairobi.org/	Nairobi.UNIC@unon.org
Lesotho	UNIC Maseru	http://maseru.unic.org	unic.maseru@unic.org
Madagascar	UNIC Antananarivo	http://antananarivo.unic.org	unic.ant@moov.mg

Namibia	UNIC Windhoek	http://windhoek.unic.org	unic.windhoek@unic.org
Nigeria	UNIC Lagos	http://lagos.unic.org	lagos@unic.org
Republic of Congo	UNIC Brazzaville	http://antananarivo.unic.org	unic.brazzaville@unic.org
Senegal	UNIC Dakar	http://dakar.unic.org	unic.dakar@unic.org
South Africa	UNIC Pretoria	http://pretoria.unic.org	unic.pretoria@unic.org
Togo	UNIC Lome	http://lome.unic.org	unic.lome@unic.org
United Republic of Tanzania	UNIC Dar es Salaam	http://daressalaam.unic.org http://www.untanzania.org	unic.daressalaam@unic.org
Zambia	UNIC Lusaka	http://lusaka.unic.org	unic.lusaka@unic.org
Zimbabwe	UNIC Harare	http://harare.unic.org	unic.harare@unic.org

AMERICAS			
COUNTRY	UNIC NAME	WEBSITE	EMAIL
Argentina	UNIC Buenos Aires	http://www.unic.org.ar	unic.buenosaires@unic.org
Bolivia	UNIC La Paz	http://www.nu.org.bo	unic.lapaz@unic.org
Brazil	UNIC Rio de Janeiro	http://unicrio.org.br/	unic.brazil@unic.org
Colombia	UNIC Bogota	http://www.nacionesunidas.org.co/	unic.bogota@unic.org
Mexico	UNIC Mexico City	http://www.cinu.mx	infounic@un.org.mx
Panama	UNIC Panama City	http://www.cinup.org	unic.panama@unic.org
Paraguay	UNIC Asuncion	http://asuncion.unic.org	unic.py@undp.org
Peru	UNIC Lima	http://www.uniclima.org.pe	unic.lima@unic.org
Trinidad and Tobago	UNIC Port of Spain	http://portofspain.unic.org	unic.portofspain@unic.org
United States	UNIC Washington D.C.	http://www.unicwash.org	unicdc@unicwash.org

MIDDLE EAST AND NORTH AFRICA

COUNTRY	UNIC NAME	WEBSITE	EMAIL
Algeria	UNIC Algiers	http://algiers.unic.org	unic.dz@undp.org
Bahrain	UNIC Manama	http://manama.unic.org	friji@un.org; lakshmy.v@unic.org
Egypt	UNIC Cairo	http://www.unic-eg.org	info@unic-eg.org
Lebanon	UNIC Beirut	http://www.unicbeirut.org	unic-beirut@un.org
Libya	UNIC Tripoli	http://tripoli.unic.org	tripoli@un.org
Morocco	UNIC Rabat	http://www.unicmor.ma	unicmor@unicmor.ma
Sudan	UNIC Khartoum	http://khartoum.unic.org	unic.sd@undp.org
Tunisia	UNIC Tunis	http://www.unictunis.org.tn	unic.tunis@unic.org
Yemen	UNIC Sana'a	http://www.unic-yem.org	unicyem@y.net.ye

ASIA AND PACIFIC

COUNTRY	UNIC NAME	WEBSITE	EMAIL
Australia	UNIC Canberra	http://www.un.org.au	unic.canberra@unic.org
Bangladesh	UNIC Dhaka	http://www.unicdhaka.org	unic.dhaka@undp.org
India	UNIC New Delhi	http://www.unic.org.in	unicindia@unicindia.org
Indonesia	UNIC Jakarta	http://www.unic-jakarta.org	unic.jakarta@unic.org
Islamic Republic of Iran	UNIC Tehran	http://www.unic-ir.org	unic.tehran@unic.org
Japan	UNIC Tokyo	http://www.unic.or.jp	unic.tokyo@unic.org
Myanmar	UNIC Yangon	http://yangon.unic.org	unic.myanmar@undp.org
Nepal	UNIC Kathmandu	http://kathmandu.unic.org	registry.np@undp.org; unic.np@undp.org
Pakistan	UNIC Islamabad	http://www.un.org.pk/unic/	unic.islamabad@unic.org
Philippines	UNIC Manila	http://www.unicmanila.org	unic.manila@unic.org
Sri Lanka	UNIC Colombo	http://colombo.unic.org	unic.lk@undp.org; unic.colombo@unic.org

EUROPE AND THE COMMONWEALTH OF INDEPENDENT STATES			
COUNTRY	UNIC NAME	WEBSITE	EMAIL
Armenia	UNO Yerevan	http://www.un.am	uno.yerevan@unic.org
Austria	UNIS Vienna	http://www.unis.unvienna.org	unis@unvienna.org
Azerbaijan	UNO Baku	http://azerbaijan.unic.org	un-dpi@un-az.org
Belarus	UNO Minsk	http://www.un.by	dpi.staff.by@undp.org
Belgium	UNRIC Brussels	http://www.unric.org	info@unric.org
Czech Republic	UNIC Prague	http://www.osn.cz	info@osn.cz
Georgia	UNO Tbilisi	http://www.ungeorgia.ge	uno.tbilisi@unic.org
Kazakhstan	UNO Almaty	http://kazakhstan.unic.org/	kazakhstan@unic.org
Poland	UNIC Warsaw	http://www.unic.un.org.pl	unic.poland@unic.org
Romania	UNIC Bucharest	http://www.onuinfo.ro	unic.romania@unic.org
Russian Federation	UNIC Moscow	http://www.unic.ru	dpi-moscow@unic.ru
Switzerland	UNIS Geneva	http://www.unog.ch	press_geneva@unog.ch
Turkey	UNIC Ankara	http://www.unicankara.org.tr	unic.ankara@unic.org
Ukraine	UNO Kyiv	http://www.un.org.ua	registry@un.org.ua
Uzbekistan	UNO Tashkent	http://www.un.uz	registry.uz@undp.org

Photo credits